*A six-week journey to finding true rest
in a pathologically busy world*

Alexander Bickerton

Copyright © 2025 Alexander R. Bickerton

1st Edition
ISBN: 978-0-646-71465-3

All rights reserved. No part of this publication may be reproduced, distributed or transmitted in any form or by any means, including photocopying, recording, or other electronic or mechanical methods, without the prior written permission of Alexander Bickerton, except in the case of brief quotations embodied in critical reviews and certain other non-commercial uses permitted by copyright law. For permission requests, email with subject line "Attention: Permissions Enquiry" at the email address below.

sandy@kuriakos.press

Unless otherwise specified, all scripture quotations are from the ESV® Bible (The Holy Bible, English Standard Version®), copyright© 2001 by Crossway Bibles, a publishing ministry of Good News Publishers. Used by permission. All rights reserved.

Scripture quotations marked (NIV) are taken from the Holy Bible, New International Version®, NIV®. Copyright © 1973, 1978, 1984, 2011 by Biblica, Inc.™ Used by permission of Zondervan. All rights reserved worldwide. www.zondervan.com The "NIV" and "New International Version" are trademarks registered in the United States Patent and Trademark Office by Biblica, Inc.™

Other scripture quotations specified are Alexander Bickerton's express translation from the original Greek Text published by United Bible Societies (UBS5) in 2015. These are marked AT (Author's Translation).

Any internet addresses (websites, blogs, etc.) in this book are offered as references for information only. They are not intended in any way to be or imply an endorsement by Alexander Bickerton, nor does Alexander Bickerton vouch for the content of these sites for the life of this book.

Chapter 4 image 'Continuous line yoke' is generated using Adobe's Firefly AI image creator tool. All other images are used by permission under a standard iStock image licence.

Cover design by Liam Berry

To the incredible people of Kenmore Church

May you find the abundant life Jesus has promised you

John 10:10

Contents

Introduction i
How to use this book iv
Digital Resources vii

Chapter 1: Soul Distress 1
   1.1 Busy is Normal 2
   1.2 What if we have accepted a lie? 10
   1.3 What if we were made for more? 20
   1.4 Weekly Reflection 28
   1.5 Group Session 32

Chapter 2: Detox 37
   2.1 What's a Soul? 38
   2.2 What's making us sick? 44
   2.3 Detox 52
   2.4 Weekly Reflection 62
   2.5 Group Session 66

Chapter 3: Reality Check 71
   3.1 Dust and Breath 72
   3.2 Time is Precious 80
   3.3 Admitting Defeat 88
   3.4 Weekly Reflection 94
   3.5 Group Session 98

Chapter 4: Paradox 103
   4.1 Jesus' Yoke 104
   4.2 Working from Rest 110
   4.3 The Place of Rest 116
   4.4 Weekly Reflection 124
   4.5 Group Session 128

Chapter 5: The Yoke of the Cross* *133
    5.1 An Uncomfortable Question 134
    5.2 A Cross for a Yoke 140
    5.3 It is Finished...148
    5.4 Weekly Reflection 158
    5.5 Group Session 162

Chapter 6: Soul Rest* *167
    6.1 A New Master 168
    6.2 When You Pray 174
    6.3 Soul Rest...182
    6.4 Weekly Reflection 188
    6.5 Group Session 192
    6.6 Where to from here? 196
    Acknowledgements...200

Introduction

My line of work is famous for people burning out. In the final semester of my first undergraduate degree, one of my lecturers welcomed me into his office and showed me a cohort photo of his graduating year. I feigned interest in the unrecognizable and slightly blurred faces as he dragged me on his nostalgic journey.

But as he pointed to each face and summarized their stories, I realized what he was doing. This one burnt out. That one had an affair. That one lost his health. Of the twenty or so individuals, only three, including my lecturer, had made it to maturity in their career. It was a warning.

Over the last thirty years, this phenomenon has worsened in Australian society. It's not just high pressure, high demand careers which are claiming people's wellbeing and stability. It seems everyone is struggling with the weight of life, regardless of age, sector, background, and religious persuasion. Very few feel like they are truly thriving.

Contemporary Australian life is conspiring to drive us to a question that humanity has been asking for centuries: is there more to life than this?

It's a question that comes from a place of disillusionment, hurt, disappointment, and weariness. It's a question that carries at its core the recognition that life lived according to the pattern we've inherited is ultimately disappointing.

Christians are not immune from finding themselves in this space. Many of the promises of Jesus are available, but don't seem to find fulfilment in our life now.

If you've picked up this book, you are probably in such a place. Life promised much but hasn't delivered, or you've been doing your best for such a long time only to discover that it hasn't borne the fruit you'd hoped. If you have a faith, it may not be living up to its hype.

Chances are, you're tired from living life at a frantic pace, and you're not alone. Our world has never moved so quickly. We've never worked so much, slept so little, and attempted to accomplish what we now do in the space of 24 hours. And so, that little question prompts us to reach for something else, because what we have at our disposal isn't working.

Jesus Christ promised that those who responded to his message would find rest for their souls. Amidst the chaos, relentlessness and anxiety of modern urban Australian life, some people have found what it is to glide through the turbulent waters like a container ship, unmoved by the monstrous waves. These people have discovered the deep and life-giving gift of Soul Rest.

If that sounds appealing, then this book is for you.

You may know nothing about Jesus, or you may have known him your whole life. You might have never set foot in a church, or you might be a Sunday regular. This book isn't written for either group specifically; it's written for anyone who feels like they are in Jesus' words, "burdened and heavy laden."

It's written for the Australian context and based in the city of Brisbane. I pastor at a church in the western suburbs of Brisbane where people are motivated, qualified and by many outward measures successful. But they are also stretched thin, time poor, tired, anxious, and close to burnout.

There is more to life than this.

How to use this book

MEET IN A GROUP WEEKLY

This is a 6-week journey of transformation, not simply a book of devotional readings. While you may choose to pick up this book and complete the readings and reflections on your own, this kind of journey is always best taken in a group setting. For that reason, this material is well suited to an existing home/small group.

If you aren't in a group, a hosting church should make new groups available for the duration of this course. As you get together, you will watch a summary video and reflect on the week's readings and your own reflections. Your group can pray for, support and help each other along the journey.

THREE READINGS WEEKLY

You can choose how to space out the readings in your week, as long as all three plus the reflection are done before the group session. Each devotional reading reflects on a saying of Jesus, mostly drawn from Matthew's gospel.

For those who know Jesus, you are already familiar with the authority and clarity of his voice. For those who are not steeped in his teaching, you will discover how unique and insightful his words are and why they have been transforming lives for nearly 2,000 years across cultures and contexts.

ONE WEEKLY REFLECTION

The reflections respond to the readings and encourage you to examine how the ideas land in your own life. These should be completed before the group session each week, as some of the discussion will depend on your reflection. Leave enough time to reflect properly.

Some of the reflections will include a call to action. These are a critical part of taking an effective journey, so do them as diligently and honestly as you can. Your group is there to support you in following through.

ALIGNED SERMON SERIES

There is also a 6-week aligned sermon series which the host church may choose to use concurrently with the course. The sermon series and the devotional and group content are complementary. You won't find them to simply repeat each other, but you won't be left behind if you are only able to engage with one or the other. They deepen and consolidate understanding, and so the best results are in facilitating both.

This provides some powerful opportunities for the local church. Firstly, the whole church can navigate the journey together. Secondly, there are built into the course powerful moments of celebration, where a church can celebrate what is happening during the course while it is happening.

INVITE YOUR FRIENDS

This content isn't only for Christians and churchgoers. People everywhere in society are struggling under the weight of a busy life, and many without the benefit of a church community. The group environment is a more accessible way for people to engage with the words of Jesus than to come along to church on a Sunday.

Soul Rest

Digital Resources

Scan the QR code to access materials:

- Group Session videos
- Sermon videos
- Sermon outlines
- Promotion video
- Explanation video

Soul Rest

CHAPTER 1
Soul Distress

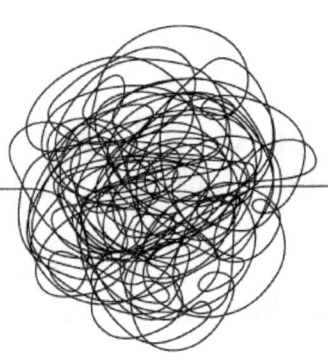

1.1

Busy is Normal

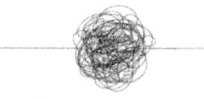

"Come to me, all who labour and are heavy-laden and I will give you rest."

Matthew 11:28

When was the last time someone asked you, "How has your week been?"

Chances are it was in the last 24 hours. And your response?

Busy...

I don't doubt it. You probably have had a busy week. You may even be attempting to multitask while reading this or squeezing it in between important tasks or a rare moment of downtime in a busy day.

Chapter 1 | Soul Distress

It's ok—you can go and do that thing you're behind on. This reading isn't going anywhere.

You're back? Alright, let's get down to business. Or should I say, busyness?

Our three kids are still young which means that rather than a 'kiss-and-run', we stay with them until the classroom doors open, which gives a few minutes every day to chat to other parents. I can't remember the last time I asked someone that question and heard something other than, "Oh busy, you?"

And it's not just parents. Company executives are busy. My barber is busy. The cleaner who comes to our house every two weeks is busy (don't judge—no tennis court, just an endless pile of laundry). Even the young adults I know are busy. It must be hard work figuring out how to spend that spare time...

I'm sure you can relate to feeling like this is the busiest we've ever been. And it's a different kind of busy to when I was early full-time career, early marriage, running an NFP as a volunteer, and giving six hours a week at my church. That was my choice. But this kind of busy seems out of my control. By the time 'big rocks' of my life like family and children, work, and the rhythms of the world around us take their ravenous bites of my schedule, there's very little left over.

And we haven't even entered the gauntlet of weekend sports.

All signs point to the fact that 'busy' is 'normal' in our society. And 'normal' means 'good'. Ever tried answering that question with, "Oh it was restful, relaxing and overall, I didn't do very much." I promise you; you will see eyebrows raised higher than the price of organic milk.

People will question what circumstances could possibly allow you that kind of rest and margin. Probably, they will feel the uncomfortable tension of despising your lack of productivity while wishing they could answer that way themselves.

But if busy is normal, and normal is good, have we slowed down long enough to ask the question: is busy *really* good?

Do you feel good when you're busy?

I don't mean do you feel accomplished when you're productive and fruitful. I mean when you're already breathless because of the pace of life and your to-do-list chooses that exact moment to give you a punch in the stomach, do you feel as though life is going according to plan?

Far from feeling good, all my worst qualities come out when I'm busy. I'm constantly telling my kids how quickly they need to do things because of how late we are. Things which should get done don't. I struggle to concentrate on one task because of the anxiety of the next task, or the limited timeframe before needing to race off to run an errand or meet an obligation. My words are sharp and my tone abrupt, and my wife and kids are the ones who suffer.

But this is normal, right? This is *good?*

Of course, working and being productive are important parts of being human. We all get tremendous satisfaction out of completing a task, ticking off a list and contributing to society. Those aren't bad things. But our penchant for productivity, combined with the acceleration of assistive technology has brought the pace of life to a frenetic level—one that our bodies are struggling under, and our souls are faring even worse.

It's no secret that there has been a mental health crisis in recent decades. Anxiety levels have been steadily on the rise since the 1950s and clinical mental health diagnosis is more prevalent than ever. In 2009, the number of Australians who experienced depression and anxiety was 11%. That's risen in 2024 to 17% of the population.[1]

The alarming trend within that rise is that those born in the 90s and onward are twice as likely to suffer from anxiety and depression as people of the same age 15 years ago.[2] People

---

[1] https://www.aihw.gov.au/mental-health/overview/prevalence-and-impact-of-mental-illness
[2] https://www.theguardian.com/society/2023/nov/28/successive-australian-generations-suffering-worse-mental-health-than-the-one-before-study-shows

born into the fast paced, interactive technology driven world we are creating are struggling more than ever.

Anxiety and depression are complex conditions affected by multiple factors including circumstances, genetics, and lifestyle. But a spiritual view understands that conditions such as these are a kind of 'soul-sickness'. It is the deepest parts of us which need healing and rest. Parts that medication, attitude and lifestyle can only partially influence.

But a First Century Jewish Rabbi claimed to not just *have* the solution, but to *be* the solution:

> *"Come to me all who labour... and I will give you rest."*

These words mean that Jesus wasn't just addressing a First Century need. He wasn't marketing a new pillow or a scenic cruise in a fishing ship along the Sea of Galilee—or starting a union. He wasn't promising detachment or mindfulness. He was offering something timeless and relevant for all people, everywhere, at any point in history. He makes it clear in the very next verse:

---

https://www.aihw.gov.au/mental-health/overview/prevalence-and-impact-of-mental-illness

Chapter 1 | Soul Distress

"... you will find rest for your souls."

What Jesus is talking about is Soul Rest. Not a holiday, not the magic 8 hours of sleep a night, not escape from the relentless struggle of existing in this world. He was offering a deep, immovable and satisfying Soul Rest.

It sounds a lot like what we need.

But like most of what Jesus offers, Soul Rest is available, but it's not automatic.

The end of each reading will include a short prayer. If you aren't used to praying, no problem. You can skip this part if it really isn't your thing. But maybe this is the right time to give it a go. Simply read out this simple prayer and believe in your heart that God is listening. If you're already familiar with prayer, use the suggested prayers as a starting point.

Prayer for today

Dear God, help me to find and receive the Soul Rest that Jesus is talking about. I ask that during this course, you would show me what steps to take to bring peace to my soul. Please begin to bring this peace to my soul today.

Amen.

Chapter 1 | Soul Distress

1.2

What if we have accepted a lie?

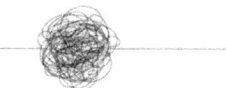

"You have heard that it was said, 'An eye for an eye and a tooth for a tooth.' But I say to you, Do not resist the one who is evil. But if anyone slaps you on the right cheek, turn to him the other also. And if anyone would sue you and take your tunic, let him have your cloak as well. And if anyone forces you to go one mile, go with him two miles."

Matthew 5:38-41

I want to introduce you to an idea called a *cultural narrative*. And by that term, I don't mean a narrative written by a culture, as thrilling as it would be to talk about Dale digging a hole and it filling with water. A narrative that displays culture can be seen in movies like the 1977 classic, *The Castle*, but we are talking about more than stories *from* a culture.

Think more *cultural narration*. If there was a narrator stitching together the various scenes of modern life in Australia, what would they say?

In one scene, the face of a man in his mid-twenties is dimly lit by the glow the fridge in the early hours of the morning. Not for the first time tonight, he finds a drink of choice and returns to his cave to the flicker of a screen where he can engage in another reality, one that's far easier than real life, where he has the respect of his mates and the in-game rank to back it up. He cracks open his drink, and as he swallows a few mouthfuls, he also swallows down that sinking feeling that his real life isn't worth all that much.

In the next scene, a successful business executive arrives home late to his expansive house after another red-eye flight. It's worth it, he reflects, since his work ensures the kids are in one of the city's most prestigious schools. Standing in the doorway of his son's room, a new trophy on the desk catches his eye. Pride quickly morphs to regret, as the true cost of his trip sinks in. "How much is my time really worth?"

A University Vice-Chancellor listens with a composed and seemingly indifferent expression as the doctor goes over her latest spade of tests. "Your heart is working too hard. Are you under any significant stress at the moment?" Her phone buzzes, displaying the name of one of the faculty heads who is having staffing trouble. She apologises to the doctor and calmly answers the call. Her expression and tone are stable as she speaks, but the heart rate monitor begins to blare warnings as the stress invisible on her face fails to hide from her body.

Morgan Freeman's voice sails over the top of the scene like a salient wind, 'This is because they all believe that their worth comes from how busy, productive and successful they are.'

Our society is made up of cultural narratives like these. They drive our decisions, determine our values and ensure that all of us end up striving to live pretty much the same busy lives as each other, with some room for individuality. But just because a society believes something doesn't make it right.

This is why history is so important, and why Winston Churchill could famously say, "Those who failed to learn from history are doomed to repeat it."

Just think of the things in recent history which used to be accepted as true and good:

- Asbestos was hailed as the miracle material for construction in post-war Australia because of its strength, fire resistant properties and cheapness.

- BPA was considered harmless in food-grade plastics, until 2023 when the European Food Safety Authority reduced the acceptable intake by a factor of 20,000 times.[3] Yes, twenty thousand. Whoops.
- And up until recently, Australia allowed kids under 16 to have social media…

The lack of health in our souls should act as a canary in the coal mine for some of these unspoken rules of society. If anxiety, loneliness and stress are the results of the world we have created for our young people, there's something we aren't doing right.

While we've learned to react to bad social narratives, they don't disappear without collateral damage, and history shows us that we often find ourselves in another, more complex disaster. What we really need is a voice that can speak not just to the present, but timelessly; one which sees below the level of action and consequence to the very soul of a human being.

We need a voice which can call out the unspoken narratives of our society which are making our souls sick and lead us in a better direction.

This is exactly the kind of voice Jesus assumes in the passage at the start of this reading. The concept of 'turning the other

---

[3] https://www.foodstandards.gov.au/consumer/chemicals/bpa

cheek' is taken directly from this counterintuitive and countercultural teaching. And while the advice is rather thought provoking, perhaps the most significant words in these verses are:

"You have heard it said... But I say to you..."

Jesus made a habit out of speaking this way. What he was saying to the First Century lower-to-middle-class, Roman-oppressed audience was:

"This world tells you one thing, but I tell you another."

Or:

"You've accepted rules from this world about how to live your life that are actually hurting you. I'm here to tell you how to find real life."

It's this posture which has made the words of a carpenter's son from Nazareth so powerful and timeless. For 2,000 years, people all around the world who have received Jesus' words find a life of spiritual soul-health which bucks the trends of their time and society.

In statements like these, Jesus hands us a map leading from our current soul-sick state to his offer of Soul Rest. It's a three-step process:

1. Identify what we have 'heard it said...'
2. Reject the cultural narrative
3. Adopt Jesus', 'But I tell you...'

So, let's imagine that instead of being born in a dirty stable in ancient Bethlehem, Jesus' mother, Mary, had to give birth in the pungent laundry room of an overcrowded Mater Hospital. Instead of preaching to thousands on the hills surrounding Jerusalem, crowds gathered at the West End markets buzzing with curiosity at a humbly dressed man who was teaching about real life in the humid open-air.

He begins to address the spoken and unspoken rules of our contemporary, urban Australian society which drive us to be so pathologically busy...

> You have heard it said, 'My worth is in my productivity'

The employee with the best results gets the promotion. Only the smartest and hardest working people achieve their dreams. If you aren't being productive, you feel wasteful, lazy and ineffective.

And rest? Well, rest is by nature incompatible with productivity (as well as a few other 'p' words: promotion, professionalism, persistence). Ergo, the one who rests has little worth.

> You have heard it said, 'You will miss out on good things if you aren't busy'

There is a world to be travelled, cuisines to sample, experiences to be had, Netflix shows which can't be missed, a stock or housing boom to ride *right now,* an unmissable opportunity... the list is endless. And the only way to do it all is by living life at a frenetic pace—not only to take it all in, but to have the money and spare time to get there in the first place.

We do this to our kids, too. And we mean well by it. But we teach them to live a busy life full of extra-curriculars because they need every opportunity. And don't forget to try your hardest *all the time.*

> You have heard it said, 'You'll have the time to rest later'

In the next season of life, once things slow down, you'll finally have the time to rest and enjoy life. Maybe in retirement. Unless you die first.

But seriously, if life is about 40-60 years of *this (insert your life here)* before getting proper rest, that seems like a bad deal. Many of our lifestyles will lead us to physical and mental peril by the time we get there, and then what's left to be enjoyed?

What if it was possible to enjoy every day, navigating this crazy world with a deep rest of your soul?

Chapter 1 | Soul Distress

The crowd leans in as the words from Jesus' mouth flow...

"But I say to you..."

You have heard it said, 'My worth is in my productivity'. But I say to you, your worth comes from the one who made you, and not from your ability to provide or other's opinions of you. (Matthew 10:31)

You have heard it said, 'You will miss out on good things if you aren't busy'. But I say to you, the best things in life come as a gift from your Heavenly Father who gives good gifts to his children. (Matthew 7:7-11)

You have heard it said, 'You'll have the time to rest later'. But I say to you, "Come to me all who labour and are heavy-laden and I will give you rest." (Matthew 11:28)

So, the question for us is this:

Am I willing to reject the statements of this world which drive me to be so busy so I can receive the Soul Rest Jesus offers?

Prayer for today

Dear God, I thank you that because you made me and consider me valuable that I don't need to find my worth in constant productivity. Help me to find my sense of worth in how you see me and not in my achievements, good deeds, or the opinions of others. Show me any of the lies I have accepted about life which prevent me from finding rest for my soul and help me to hear your voice.

Amen.

Chapter 1 | Soul Distress

1.3
What if we were made for more?

When Jesus heard this, he said to him, "You still lack one thing. Sell everything you have and give to the poor, and you will have treasure in heaven. Then come, follow me."

Luke 18:22 NIV

Actor and comedian Jim Carrey once said, "I wish everyone could get rich and famous and have everything they ever dreamed of, so they will know it's not the answer."

Those are the kind of words that seem meaningful and evoke a solemn "mmmm", before effortlessly drifting away like a dandelion seed caught in the wind. But if we considered them awhile, they might sink a bit deeper into our souls.

Chapter 1 | Soul Distress

What do you want in life? What do you wake up in the morning considering, 'that's a worthy goal'? What would happen if you got hold of it—all of it? What would your life look like?

Go on, think about it for a moment.

There are very few people who could say they got 'everything they ever dreamed of.' A small percentage of the human race manages to succeed so well in life that they can literally tick off every dream and desire they could want. While much of the world's population struggles at the other end of the spectrum with little agency and choice in their lives, chances are, if you're reading this, you're caught somewhere in the middle.

Successful enough to have motivating goals.

Not so successful that they're all within your power right now.

Greyhounds hunting a mechanical rabbit.

But everyone's desires are different. Some only want pleasure and ease in life. Some want power and control. Others just want to be unremarkable and comfortable. Many want good things: a stable family, loving relationships, satisfaction and purpose in whatever work they have found to do.

What if people like Jim Carrey simply wanted the wrong kind of stuff?

But there are two problems to the argument that simply desiring *the right* things will lead to satisfaction. Firstly, you'll never know until you achieve them all. How's that going? Secondly, Jim's not alone. Every person who has done it comes to the same conclusion: it's not enough.

So long as we are caught chasing fulfilment in our desires, we are trapped in one of two realities: chasing satisfaction, or dissatisfied.

It's at this point that we can make the choice: keep spinning in frantic circles or listen to the words of a dog who caught his own tail.

Jim's conclusion is almost identical to the story from the verse above, known as the story of the Rich Young Ruler. But there's one key difference.

The young man approached Jesus with the question, "What must I do to inherit eternal life?"

Straight off the bat, we might say that this young man's desires are in the right place. He understands that life isn't all about the here and now, but he's aware of eternity. That difference should give him a big advantage, right?

For context, this young man was a raging success in all areas of life. He was wealthy, respected, and had a squeaky-clean record. He hadn't lived a life of vanity and indulgence, nor had he made his fortune from exploitation or evil. He was in fact, a picture of first-century propriety.

The conversation continued as Jesus reiterated the commandments to him. All the basic stuff. Drive the speed limit, don't cheat on your taxes, don't steal things. As well as the advanced stuff. Honour your parents, be respectful, love God.

The man replied, 'I've done all those things ever since I was a kid.'

And here's where the conversation gets really interesting (verse 22 above). Jesus said despite all of that, despite your wealth, success, prestige, and even your religious credentials, you still lack one thing. The solution? Deny everything... and follow me.

Before we try to swallow the significance of that, let's just observe *why* the conversation happened at all. The young man had done everything right, buying into every positive cultural narrative around him and exceeding expectations. So, why did he need to ask this question? Surely, of all people, he already knew the answer to eternal life?

But the fact he even asked this question shows an intuitive awareness that all he had done was not enough. He still did not have the confidence that it guaranteed him eternal life. Add him to the list of people through history who 'made it' far enough to realise 'making it' isn't the point.

And if the young man was intuitively aware of the fact, Jesus had the authority and insight to call it out: 'You're missing something.' And it was a big something. Something so significant that the only way to get it was to give away everything he had.

In this statement, Jesus turns upside down everything this young man had learned from the society around him, including the religious teachers. And they are cultural narratives that humanity and our society still follow today. The narratives say that the only pathway to 'eternal life' (or a satisfied soul, spiritual significance, meaning and purpose, or just *real rest*—take your pick) is through *having* things and *doing* things.

Our society works the same way. But sadly, *having* and *doing* are pale shadows of what it means to be a human *being.* Jesus' recommendation to the one who wants eternal life, the deep satisfaction of soul that ultimately all of us were designed to pursue, is to follow him.

If we accept Jesus' point here, then many of the cultural narratives our world offers us aren't just missing the mark, they're leading us astray. What if following Jesus isn't just an add-on to a life of success and fulfilment by following our cultural narratives? What if following Jesus *is* a life of success and fulfilment?

In Matthew's version of this story, Jesus says to the young man, "*If you want to be complete*, go and sell your possessions and give to the poor, and you will have treasure in heaven; and come, follow me" (Matthew 19:21 NIV).

The two phrases mean the same thing. You lack something. You're incomplete. So, where is completeness really found? What is completeness?

If all the cultural narratives we swallow are an attempt to meet this deep and unidentified incompleteness, they've continually come up short. They fill us up with the desire to have stuff, to do stuff, to achieve and receive the reputation and opinion-based success that goes along with it.

But what if we were made for more? What if the answer to the deep, unfulfilled pieces of our frantic and incomplete souls cannot be found in any of our cultural narratives?

What if the only way to discover peace, rest and fulfilment is to let Jesus diagnose our souls and to follow him?

Prayer for today

Dear God, help me today to see my life for what it is. Show me what I hold to be important and how it compares to what Jesus offers. Give me the courage to listen to what Jesus says about my life and choices. Continue to lead me towards your soul rest.

Amen.

Chapter 1 | Soul Distress

1.4

Weekly Reflection

How do I feel when I'm not being productive, or when interruptions force me to change my plans?

_____

_____

_____

_____

_____

_____

_____

_____

Chapter 1 | Soul Distress

How would the people closest to me (spouse, kids, family, close friends) describe my relationship with work?

_____

_____

_____

_____

_____

_____

What unspoken rules drive my life? Perhaps they were modelled in my family growing up.

_____

_____

_____

_____

_____

_____

Soul Rest

Am I happy with how busy my life is? Why/why not?

_____

_____

_____

_____

_____

_____

What is the most important one or two goals for me in life—the core things I would regret not doing well?

_____

_____

_____

_____

_____

_____

If I continued to live life the way I am now, will this goal be achieved? Would the cost be worthwhile?

_____

_____

_____

_____

_____

_____

_____

_____

_____

_____

_____

_____

_____

_____

1.5

Group Session

Welcome to the Soul Rest Group discussions. It's possible that you are in a pre-existing group picking up this material. It's also possible that you're in a new group with new people you may not be familiar with.

Either way, these group times will be some of the most meaningful parts of the experience. During this time, you will have the opportunity to debrief from the weekly readings and message, share your thoughts and hear how others have responded to the material. You will also have the opportunity to deepen friendships, find support and comfort each other through life.

It's important to start by developing a group understanding. The point of a setting like this is to be able to share with vulnerability and no judgement, with confidence and with trust.

Chapter 1 | Soul Distress

If you're part of a new group, spend some time with an icebreaker to get to know each other a little bit. Here are some suggestions:

- Two truths and a lie
- Would you rather…
- One Word (say the first word that comes into your mind in response to another word or idea)

OUR GROUP DEAL

Choose five values/commitments to make to each other for the duration of the course.

1. _____

2. _____

3. _____

4. _____

5. _____

DISCUSSION QUESTIONS

1. How did you find the readings this week?

2. What stood out to you the most?

3. On a scale of 1 to 10, with 1 being the least busy and 10 being the busiest you've ever been, where does your life rank currently?

4. What would you say are the cultural narratives which inform your life?

5. What elements of your life bring you the most satisfaction?

6. On a scale of 1 to 10, with 1 being the worst and 10 the best, how rested do you feel? Try to examine on a deeper level than simply physical rest. Think about your levels of anxiety, stress, and ability to maintain resilience, calm and to be satisfied with your circumstances.

7. Do you feel as though there is more to life than you experience right now?

At the end of each group session, it is important to spend some time praying with one another. Prayer is not only something we can do individually, but people have been praying together publicly for thousands of years. It gives us the chance to support and care for each other, to share any needs.

Pray for each other

- To get the most out of the course
- To begin to feel more rested and satisfied
- To reflect deeply and honestly
- To have any other needs met

Soul Rest

CHAPTER 2

Detox

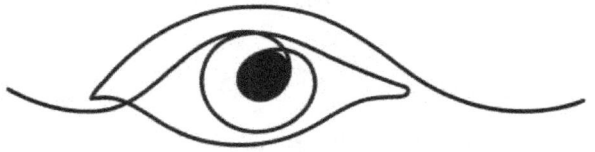

2.1

What's a Soul?

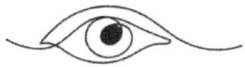

*Take my yoke upon you, and learn from me, for I am gentle and lowly in heart, and you will find **rest for your souls**.*

Matthew 11:29

It's unusual in our context to think too much about your soul. Did your teacher talk about it in school? Not mine. Cover it in your science, marketing, math, law or language degree? Nope. Has your boss scheduled a PD on looking after your soul?

Unless you've gotten into some Eastern Meditation, religion, or out-there yoga class, you're probably not used to thinking or talking about your soul.

The closest thing in our society is what the kids these days are calling 'vibes' and 'energy'. And from the little of that I actually understand, it's not even close to the inward dimension of your existence which Plato described as the unbodied seat of our desires, intellect and contemplation.

But while you may or may not have thought extensively about it, everyone, bar a few extreme viewpoints, intuitively acknowledges that there is something within us that is more than just a brain driving a flesh suit in pursuit of procreation and survival. There are too many abstract tendencies and experiences of human beings which separate us from animals that can't be justified by an evolutionary, survival-of-the-fittest philosophy.

Why do we create art? Why does beauty take our breath away? Why do we feel compassion for things weaker and smaller than us? Why do we seek to leave a legacy or remember the past? The list goes on.

Let's try and avoid the mire of philosophy's attempt to define and understand the soul and just cut straight to the chase:

You have a body.

You have a soul.

They affect each other.

They each have needs.

Make sense?

This is the way the Bible teaches that we were created. Back in the book of Genesis we see the story of God creating the first people. Every other creature God simply spoke into existence.

Let there be fish.

Boom.

Fish exist.

Let there be an awkwardly tall rhomboid-shaped animal with a neck as long as its body. And make it yellow with orange spots.

Boom.

Giraffes exist.

But with man, God had a special method:

> *"Then the LORD God formed the man of dust from the ground and breathed into his nostrils the breath of life, and the man became a living creature."*
>
> *Genesis 2:7*

God took the dust of the ground and got his hands dirty forming the first man. The thing that brought him to life was the breath of God. And the word used for *breath* also means *spirit*. There was something literally spiritual about the creation of the human race.

Ever since, humanity has existed in the tension between being physical, formed from the dust, and spiritual, carrying the very breath of God in our lungs.

Dust and breath. That's what we are.

It's why we can marvel at something. It's why we can fall in love. It's why we and not the dolphins or the crows rule this earth.

But we also bleed. We get tired. We sweat. We fall sick and die. Dust and breath.

So, the implication of Jesus' words in the today's verse is that the heavy and wearisome burdens we carry in life are ones that don't just require physical rest. They require a spiritual rest to find relief. They require a rest for our souls.

How do we rest our souls?

Humanity has come up with many attempts at finding this rest. Meditation, or the less mystical, more palatable modern equivalent, 'mindfulness', would be the most well-known. Many philosophies and even religions have been created with some form of soul rest as the ultimate goal.

Buddhism aims at Nirvana, a state of inner peace which is achieved by detachment from all our physical parts to release our spiritual part to peace. Hindu Moksha is much the same, release from suffering by shedding the physical self and transcending to be an entirely spiritual being.

Even the prevailing Western religion of *Retirementism,* through the spiritual discipline of *Superannuation,* aims at escaping the rat race to find ultimate rest soaking up rays on the Whitsundays shoreline.

But none of these is in view in Jesus' words. The path to Soul Rest is in simply coming to Jesus. In coming, we are promised that he will give us rest for our souls. It isn't a release from our physical reality as in the Eastern religions. It is in a redemption of our physical reality by healing us spiritually.

You see, in coming to Jesus we are actually returning to the one who created our soul. The breath within us longs to be reunited with the one who breathed it into us. It longs to find God. True rest for our souls is found not in escaping the world, but in returning to the God who created this world and us.

But as you've probably guessed by how tired and burdened you still feel, it's not quite that automatic. That's why this week is about what is making our souls sick and how to shake it with Jesus' help.

Chapter 2 | Detox

Prayer for today

Dear God, thank you that you made me with your breath. Thank you that you have given me worth and meaning far more than I could have hoped or expected. I ask this week you would give me a greater sense of your love for me as one who carries your breath inside me. Help me to be open to what changes may be needed in my life to find rest.

Amen.

2.2

What's making us sick?

What good does it do to gain the whole world but to lose one's soul? What shall a man give in return for his soul?

Matthew 16:26 AT

A lovably flawed protagonist who is filled with a desire for something unattainable is suddenly assailed by a horned character sporting a pointy tail, pitchfork and a red cape. The Devil makes a nearly irresistible offer to grant the one thing their heart desires.

The only cost?

Their soul.

Chapter 2 | Detox

The Phantom of the Opera, the 2000 release starring Brendan Fraser, *Bedazzled*, and Disney's *The Little Mermaid* are some popular examples of this common trope. Even 19th Century violin virtuoso and composer, Niccolò Paganini, was so remarkably talented, that persistent rumours spread of him selling his soul to the Devil in exchange for his other-worldly musical skill.

When we think of someone 'losing their soul', this is almost exclusively the scenario that comes to mind. Our assumption is then that the only person who may be so unlucky is, in the words of Ursula the Sea Witch, *those poor unfortunate souls* who by some personal flaw or need made the well-intentioned but dire mistake of trading that which they cannot hope to regain.

But Jesus, who clearly pre-dates both Hollywood trope and the medieval conceptualisation of the Devil, says there is a far more common way to lose one's soul than to sell it to the *Enemy* (Greek: diabolos).

His credentials here are pretty good. Not only is Jesus, as we have argued, the authority on our souls, but the Devil literally offered to give him the world in exchange for his soul twelve chapters earlier. It's with that 40-day-fast-fueled victory under his belt that he can speak so authoritatively:

Soul Rest

> *Then Jesus said to his disciples, "If any of you wants to follow after me, let him abandon his own way, take up his cross and follow after me. [25]If you desire to hang onto your soul, you will lose it. But whoever loses his soul for my sake will find it. [26]For what will it benefit you if you gain the whole world but your soul is given away? What can you give in exchange for your soul?*
>
> *Matthew 16:24-26 AT*

The picture Jesus presents is not one of a single, tragic transaction where a bad decision bears eternal consequence. Neither is he talking about a single redeeming moment of conversion. It's a picture of pursuit. He connects the losing or saving of our soul with the pursuit of following either him or the world.

And while the gospel can give a person assurance of the safety of their soul, we are still able to, by choices and actions in this life, experience what losing our soul feels like. Otherwise, Jesus' Soul Rest would indeed be automatic (and you would have stopped reading last week). Pursue the world, and you will feel your soul slipping away. Pursue Jesus, and he will give you rest.

So, what does it look like to pursue the world? And what's so bad about it? Do we all need to withdraw to the mountains, renounce possessions and career and live in a monastery?

Here's where we make a bit of a leap—but bear with me. It's very, very important.

Pursuing the world in our context looks like *being and feeling busy.*

All the cultural narratives we have accepted are driven fundamentally by the desire to pursue things in the world. Yes, possessions, comforts, achievements, etc. We're told that those things will eventually lead us to happiness, peace and... *rest.*

Why else would we be so consumed in chasing them? Why else would humans continue to run recklessly into the circumstances which are causing anxiety, stress and sickness to skyrocket? It's because we genuinely believe that by effort and commitment, and with some calculated (and uncalculated) sacrifice, we really can make it. We can have everything. We can *gain the world.*

Before we let Jesus' words address this again, we must acknowledge that there are three types of people reading this right now.

The first type might be those who have lived a life without too much thought or concern for the condition of their souls. That's a normal place to be. Perhaps some of you feel as though you are waking up to parts of yourself previously unknown, and now realising how important looking after your soul is. Chances are, you're trying to find a way to slow down to cope with life.

The second type are those who have been aware of the need to look after their soul and may have tried routes other than Christianity. You may have even found many of these things helpful and feel as though they have improved your soul health. Many of them bear similarity to the teachings of Jesus. But one important distinction is how exclusive Jesus' presentation is. It's not about mindfulness, meditation, or good karma. It's about following Jesus, or not.

The third type might be those who are familiar with Jesus and have already expressed the desire to be his 'follower' (just another way of saying a *Christian*). You're aware of your soul and the need to take care of it. Jesus is important to you and following him is key. But you probably also feel unhappily busy. Our cultural narratives still influence you.

To the first type of person, there is a fundamental shift that needs to happen before it is possible to find rest for your soul. Your ultimate goal, that which is your life pursuit, needs to shift from things which are temporary to things that are eternal. From looking after your body to looking after your *soul and* body.

Ascending the corporate ladder, achieving your dreams and raising a functional family won't save your soul. Neither will donating to charity, always returning your shopping trolley

Chapter 2 | Detox

and driving a Tesla. The only way to save your soul and to receive the rest it so desperately needs is to reconnect with the one who made it. Only once that journey begins will the soul sickness caused by any manner of things start to disappear.

To the second type of person, there is an immovable bollard in the middle of the road at this point. It cannot be escaped that Jesus' claims are exclusive. One cannot follow Jesus and another spiritual authority. And so, all there is to say here is that Jesus' teachings are there to be tested. Either he will prove himself, or not.

To the third type of person, Jesus' words are no less significant. While you have chosen to set your life trajectory in pursuit of Jesus, all the same things in this life are constantly trying to draw your soul away from a life of connection with him. Jesus may have your soul eternally, but you can still experience soul sickness when the busyness of the world captures your soul.

Now, returning to Jesus' words, what does he say about this pursuit?

He says that gaining the world is the same thing as *losing your soul*. You can't have both.

Let's try it another way:

Soul sickness is what it feels like to be losing your soul.

Right, but how is this applying to me, again?

Engaging in activities, intentionally or not, which make your soul sick is exactly how you lose your soul.

Okay—but that only applies if I'm not a Christian, right? Aren't we talking here about eternal security? Nope. Christians don't find themselves immune to anxiety, depression, or illness of any kind. *You can be saved and not know rest.*

While a Christian may have a powerful set of driving principles, it's possible to still drive down the wrong road and experience the consequences. Having a life raft doesn't mean you don't feel the waves.

Once more, a little closer to home:

You are giving your soul away to whatever makes you busy.

And here we are. The reason busyness is so toxic. The reason Jesus said you are either trying to preserve your soul by pursuing the world or to leave it to God by pursuing Jesus. It's because these things which capture our time and demand our attention are starving us from the connection we so desperately need with our creator.

It's impossible to be both busy and connected to God.

So, what's making you busy?

Is it worth giving your soul to?

Prayer for today

Dear Lord, help me to see where my life is going. Show me the result of the things I am pursuing. Help me to make the changes necessary to pursue you, Jesus.

Amen.

2.3

Detox

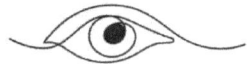

If your right eye causes you to stumble, gouge it out and throw it away. It is better for you to lose one part of your body than for your whole body to be thrown into hell. [30] *And if your right hand causes you to stumble, cut it off and throw it away. It is better for you to lose one part of your body than for your whole body to go into hell.*

Matthew 5:29-30 NIV

I'm one of the 88% of the Australian population who, by natural endowment, is free to indulge in the hero of flavour in the modern Western diet known as *gluten*. While levels of intolerance to the substance have grown significantly over recent decades, my genetics seem to have escaped unscathed.

But like all my gluten-loving brothers and sisters, I know plenty of people who have to take extra care around food. A handful of them can't even have a trace of the substance, or they spend the next 12 hours resembling someone who chose the wrong food vendor on the streets of Delhi.

Jesus' words here seem rather dramatic—and they're meant to be. Our wincing while reading them would have been matched by the gasps of those who heard him say it. Gouge out your eye and throw it away?? Cut off your hand??

The modern audience probably reacts more strongly to the mention of 'hell' than of self-dismemberment. But the former statement, and not the mention of hell, (originally *Gehenna*, a Hebrew word for the local Valley of Hinnom[4]), would have been what set his hearers ablaze.

We must understand that Jesus was being intentionally provocative here. There is no time in history where the accepted understanding of this passage is that we are instructed to literally mutilate our bodies in this way. But the impact of what he says must be appreciated.

What's the first change that someone with a celiac diagnosis makes? Their diet. Having discovered that gluten, or dairy, or any food is physically causing us to be sick, it would be insane

---

[4] BDAG γεένα (2000, p190)

to not address it by eliminating, or at the very least limiting the foods which cause it.

This is the implication of Jesus' teaching about sin. He teaches that sin isn't simply a violation of some trivial whim of a God who wants unreasonable control over our lives. The real issue with sin is that it *harms us* and those around us. That's why God made prohibitions in the first place. Not to ruin our fun, but to allow us to live a healthy life—not just physically, but spiritually, too.

So, when Jesus identifies lust as a dangerous activity, it's because of the damage that lust can lead to. It's not hard to argue the point. Affairs start with lust. Casual hookups prioritise lust over the deeper human needs of security and ongoing connection. In the case of Old Testament hero, King David, lust led to both adultery and murder.

Our society has a whole industry built on lust and while it lurks in the shadows away from sight, a 2015 study in Melbourne showed that pornography has its black tentacles grasping at 99% of Australian men under 30, and 85% of women of the same age.[5] The statistics are terrifying, and the links to poor sexual and mental health are clear. Once again, it's the tech-affected generations who are suffering most.

---

[5] https://onlinelibrary.wiley.com/doi/full/10.1111/1753-6405.12678

So, Jesus isn't trying to ruin our fun. He's trying to help us swim against the tide of soul-destroying habits. What he's saying is that if we really knew what we were doing to both our bodies and our souls through behaviours like these, we would cut them off immediately.

At this point, it's useful to take stock of your own life and habits to identify if indeed there are any destructive or unhealthy behaviours which are preventing you from finding Soul Rest. It could be things like recreational drug use, an unhealthy relationship with alcohol, an addiction to gambling, or even a damaging personal relationship.

There are many reasons we let these behaviours slide in our lives. We think we have control over them. We justify them by saying they meet our needs, whether that's because our bodily needs aren't getting met elsewhere, or we just can't seem to relax without them. But an honest and sober reflection is usually very clear.

Perhaps it's a festering wound of bitterness, an inescapable dependence on people's opinions of you, or a crippling self-doubt which seems to return at the worst times like an unwanted internet salesman. These are harder to detox from, but no less transformative. They don't rely on practical decisions so much as conscious direction of where you let your mind lead you.

So, give it a go—is there anything in my life that when I am truly honest with myself, I know is unhealthy?

If you've struggled to address behaviours like this in the past, you're in the right place. This is where knowing Jesus really makes a difference. A heartfelt prayer, a dose of courage and vulnerability, and the support of a community of people (like your small group) could be the key to kicking some of these in your life.

But you may be thinking, I haven't got any of those, yet I still feel like something is holding me back, spiritually. Well, now it's time to lay hands on a theme we have dabbled in over the last couple of weeks and drag it into the harsh light of the interview room, detective style.

Which demographic is consistently worse-off when it comes to indicators of soul health, as we have discussed?

Young people.

Specifically, those who have been raised in a world where interactive technology is at the centre. You know how all the oldies are complaining about kids these days, not being outside, not playing with neighbours, glued to their screens?

Chapter 2 | Detox

It turns out, that's not just geriatric melancholy. They're right.

For all the benefits of smart phones, the internet, and the information-ready, globally connected world we live in, research upon research shows that improper use of technology, smart phones in particular, is damaging our brains.

And what you may not be aware of is that it's harming us spiritually, too. Let me explain briefly, though there is a growing body of work out there which can do it much better than I can.[6]

Internet users in Australia are predominantly using YouTube and Facebook.[7] You may think platforms like these make their money through advertising, but they make their money by selling your attention. And how is your attention measured? Your time.

You are giving your time for free to these platforms and they are selling it to the highest bidder.

"What's the big deal, then? I give it willingly."

---

[6] I recommend John Mark Comer's *The Ruthless Elimination of Hurry*
[7] https://www.statista.com/statistics/1112522/australia-average-time-per-person-spent-on-selected-websites/

That's the issue—no, you don't. Or at least, the younger you are, the less control you have.

The founding president of Facebook, Sean Parker, who, tellingly, himself abstains from social media, describes how all the platforms are built to "consume as much of your time and conscious attention as possible" and they do so by "exploiting a vulnerability in human psychology."[8]

"God knows what it's doing to our children's brains."[9]

But we're now starting to see what it does to our brains and bodies. It reduces our attention span and causes us to live in a constant state of rushing and anxiety. Two cardiologists, recognizing the effects of busyness on the heart in the 70's, referred to this condition as 'hurry sickness'. This sickness had been burning in our busy society for decades before the smartphone dowsed it in rocket fuel.[10]

It behaves like any other addiction. It calls to us constantly, asking to be picked up, looked at, consumed.

---

[8] https://www.axios.com/2017/12/15/sean-parker-unloads-on-facebook-god-only-knows-what-its-doing-to-our-childrens-brains-1513306792
[9] ibid.
[10] Friedman, M. and Rosenman, R. *Type A Behavior and Your Heart*. 1974.

Don't believe me? Do you think we as a country are in control of our smart phone usage?

Well, it may surprise you to know that Australia is one of the most saturated populations when it comes to the smartphone, with 88% of all pockets/handbags sporting an AI enhanced, neurologically optimized time thief.

We're finally beating the US at something (64%).[11]

And it's a problem. 61% of Australian drivers admitted to driving while using their phone despite it being illegal.[12] Does that sound like we have it under control?

It's the first thing we look at in the morning, the last thing at night. It feels weird to go to the loo without your smartphone. Seriously, how did people ever poop without a micro-hit of dopamine every seven seconds?

Anecdotally, I once asked my year 9 students to show their screen time over a two-week holiday period. The class average was 9 hours per day for two weeks. The highest two-week average was 19 hours *per day*.

---

[11] https://pmc.ncbi.nlm.nih.gov/articles/PMC6422909/
[12] ibid.

Soul Rest

Many of us would like to be less attached to our smart phones, but it's just too hard. Not only does modern life rely on them, but bluntly, we're more addicted than we want to admit.

It's possibly the main reason we are so busy. We can be 'switched on' and 'working' all the time. More than that, it compels us to live life at a frantic pace, and we need to understand that a hurried life leads to a hurried soul, and a hurried soul is sick.

The net effect is that the brain and behavioural changes act as a spiritual tranquiliser. When you're constantly busy, you're spiritually numb.

Jesus said, "Come to me and I will give you rest." But we can't come to him because we're involuntarily too busy. And we can't accept his rest because we've allowed ourselves to be rewired internally.

Even when we drag ourselves into his presence, our mind doesn't slow down and the one thing we can't give him is our attention.

What do we do?

The same thing as the Celiac. The same thing Jesus recommends.

Detox.

"If one thing in your life—*even a good thing*— causes your soul harm..."

Prayer for today

Dear God, help me to slow down in this moment and recognize your presence. You are here with me now and you always have been. I'm pretty sure that _____ is a problem in my life and causing me to be sick. Please help me to take steps to overcome it.

Amen.

2.4

Weekly Reflection

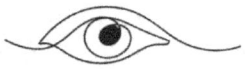

Take this brief spiritual health check. Next to each statement, write a number from 1 to 5 indicating:

1 – Never true
2 – Occasionally true
3 – Regularly true
4 – Frequently true
5 – Always true

I feel anxious	_____
I don't know how I'm going to cope with what I need to do in the day	_____
I miss deadlines, personal messages or events	_____
I spend time more time than I would like on technology	_____
I feel like I'm always busy	_____

Chapter 2 | Detox

I often feel too tired or busy to follow through with spiritual practices like prayer, attending church, or reading the Bible   _____

My self-talk is often negative   _____

I feel like I can't concentrate as well as I used to   _____

I don't usually think about God's love for me   _____

I connect my worth and identity to things that have nothing to do with God   _____

Score out of 50   _____

A score of 20 or less indicates good soul health. The higher your score, the more signs there are of soul distress in your life.

How do I feel about my score?

_____

_____

_____

_____

Soul Rest

Are there things I've let into my life that I know aren't healthy?

_____

_____

_____

_____

_____

_____

If there was one habit or behaviour I could detox from over the next 4 weeks, what would it be?

_____

_____

_____

_____

_____

_____

Chapter 2 | Detox

What would it look like to detox from it?

_____
_____
_____
_____
_____
_____
_____
_____
_____
_____
_____
_____
_____
_____
_____
_____

2.5

Group Session

This week we have laid our hands on the true problem with being busy, and some of the factors of our day and age which maximise this issue. Busyness, or more accurately, living a life that makes you feel busy and hurried, acts as a spiritual tranquiliser. It numbs our souls from finding the connection and rest they need.

If you're older than 25, you know all too well that living a healthy life doesn't happen by accident. When youth, energy and a fast metabolism abandon you, suddenly life starts to win the tug-of-war against your health. Without intentional and diligent management of your habits, the ability to enjoy life can slip away.

This is even more true spiritually than physically, because often we miss the spiritual cues. Heed this: detox is a make-or-break component of this journey to Soul Rest.

DISCUSSION QUESTIONS

1. What did you think of this week's readings?

2. What stood out to you the most?

3. What was your spiritual health score?

4. What was something you identified you would benefit from reducing or detoxing from altogether?

Technology isn't all bad, but it's one of the primary challenges of life in the modern world. Certain types of technology are riskier to use than others, such as social media, smart phones, addictive video gaming, and attention-based scrolling apps. Other elements are more explicitly sinister, such as pornography, monetised addictive apps, and platforms which make users vulnerable to exploitation, grooming or the like.

5. What is the impact of technologies such as these on your household? What would you change if you could?

6. What do you think about the idea that these things cause us to be spiritually numb?

Make a plan to support each other in detoxing from at least one negative behaviour during this course. Your group facilitator may like to write down your goal and encourage everyone to be praying for and supporting your group members.

Pray for each other:

- To gain back control over the unhealthy aspects of life
- To be courageous in identifying the real issues for the sake of soul health

Chapter 2 | Detox

Soul Rest

CHAPTER 3
Reality Check

3.1

Dust and Breath

I am the vine, and you are the branches. The one who abides in me and lets me abide in them will bear much fruit, since separate from me, you aren't able to produce anything.

John 15:5 AT

Do you know someone whom you would call a *green thumb*? Whatever the opposite is of that, I'm it. These thumbs are as black as the Prime-Minister's BMW 7-series. Plants see these thumbs coming and get their wills in order.

But I have a few friends who are genuinely green thumbs. When it comes to plants, they just get it. They know which branches to trim, what time to water, what kind of fertiliser works best. And when it comes to bearing fruit, there's a clear difference between my longsuffering mandarin tree (which I used to pick green, thinking they were limes) and their fruit gardens. My fruit grows in spite of my attention or lack thereof, but theirs is abundant and full of flavour.

The removal of negative environmental factors (so my learned friends tell me) is the easy and obvious step in caring for a plant. Get rid of the weeds competing for the nutrients. Keep nasty bugs, bats and bacteria away. But the harder step, the one that requires knowledge and patience, is creating positive conditions that allow a plant to thrive.

Last week we made a start at the first step in looking after your soul, the straightforward and obvious removal of harmful factors. This week, we are looking at the more challenging second step. What is it that your soul needs?

To revisit the Bible's description of our soul's architecture, we are a tension between dust and breath. We are physical, of this earth, which includes all the pain and limitations that go along with it. And we are spiritual, each of us carrying the breath of God which animates us.

One great difference between Christianity and the other world religions is that for the most part, other religions consider this tension as something to resolve, whereas a proper understanding of Jesus teaches us that it is a condition to be embraced.

Hindu Moksha and Buddhist Nirvana (and numerous offshoots of these philosophies) have more or less the same endpoint. The enlightened soul is one who has achieved a separation of spirit and body. They have diminished physical needs and desires to the extent that their soul is no longer affected by them. Essentially, they become purely spirit, and they escape the cycle of Samsara.[13]

Even early philosophy such as Plato elevated the mind, believing it was more fundamental to one's existence than the body. According to Plato, philosophers were the only ones who got 'close to God' by pursuit of intellect.[14] Sounds like something a philosopher would say…

On the flip side of that coin, most approaches to life which reject or only nominally acknowledge God end up pursuing the physical aspects of life as the ultimate, neglecting the spiritual. Life is all about success, achievements, legacy, fame, money, power, health—you name it. Anything but God or a healthy soul.

But the common flaw is that all these patterns of understanding seek to resolve the tension between dust and

---

[13] The cycle of life, death and rebirth according to Buddhist and Hindu belief.
[14] This is a generalisation of Platonic belief, but it is most clearly seen in *Phaedo* (249c), part of his *Dialogues*.

breath by separating body and spirit instead of finding a way for them to be happily united. Jesus didn't ask us to neglect our bodies or to ascend to a higher existence. He said,

"Abide in me."

I like that word, *abide*. It's uncommon enough that it's meaningful to say. Really, it means 'stay', or 'remain'. But somehow, for me, those words don't capture the profoundness of Jesus when he tells us to *abide in him* in the same way that a branch *abides* in the vine.

What choice does the branch have? How can it choose whether to remain in the vine or not? The moment it's not connected to the vine, it ceases to be a branch. It's just a twig. So how can the branch choose to stay?

And that's exactly Jesus' point. He isn't just giving one solution to a healthy life. He's saying that abiding in the vine is the only way to be alive at all. You were created by him, and he is the sustainer of your life. The more disconnected from him you are, the less you will feel like you are alive. Really alive. Not just breathing and existing from day to day, but fulfilled, satisfied, *rested.*

So, what does it look like to be connected to the vine? How can we abide in him?

Firstly, prayer is one of the most important ways of abiding in Jesus. In the same way that communication is the lifeblood of a relationship, prayer keeps the blood flow between vine and branch open (sap-flow doesn't sound right).

Secondly, reading the Bible and reflecting on it, as you have been doing each reading, is another effective way to abide.

Thirdly, spend time together with others who are also 'abiding in the vine'.

There are not only tonnes of different ways to connect to God, but plenty of variation in how you might approach each one. And here's a spoiler—God doesn't care that much about you 'doing it right', so long as you're doing it.

These activities all fall under a category called 'spiritual disciplines'. They're important because they meet the needs of a soul within the limitations of a body—the dust and breath tension. But the disciplines in themselves have no power. They are simply a container for the real thing, life and connection with the God who made you. They are a hose which allows the water to flow from its source to our souls.

Here's where the real power comes from. Jesus didn't *only* say abide in me. He said,

"Let me abide in you."

That's the thing about a branch. It doesn't have to think about remaining in the vine. It's not a forced discipline or regular habit. It's a reality purely because the branch already finds itself in the vine. The branch has total, natural trust in the vine to be its sustainer. And with that open invitation, the life-giving nutrients fill the branch, producing fruit.

So, there is a two-way element to this abiding, which is not only that you give yourself to Jesus, but that you receive Jesus into yourself. And that is a step of trust. Jesus won't go where he's not welcome and accepted. He gives you the dignity of that choice. But we cannot presume to receive his rest if we don't receive him by putting our faith in him.

What about the person who knows Jesus, but doesn't feel like their life is being sustained through every gruelling day and anxious fear? Am I simply telling you to pray more, read your Bible and go to church?

Yes, but—such a statement is unhelpful. We need the context of the rest of this week before the suggestion to adopt spiritual disciplines is any help at all.

For now, contemplate the following points:

- Detoxing from negative factors is only the first step to finding Jesus' Soul Rest.
- Opening the flow of life by abiding in Jesus, the Vine, requires intentional steps which are often only made possible by the first detox step. No matter how much you want to abide, you won't be able to while those barriers exist.
- Addressing the needs of your soul must be done through the abilities and limitations of a body. You are not a spirit who has a body. You are a body-and-spirit being made by God.
- Is learning to abide important enough to you that you would be willing to make some changes in your life?

Prayer for today

Dear God, thank you that you are my creator and the sustainer of my life. Regardless of my past, I would like to put my trust in you afresh today. Help me to learn to abide in Jesus and to let Jesus abide in me. I invite you to work in the parts of my inward life that might still be preventing rest.

Amen.

Chapter 3 | Reality Check

3.2

Time is Precious

"I tell you, don't be anxious about your life, whether it's what you will eat or drink, nor about what clothes you will put on your body. Is your life not more than food, and your body more than clothes?

27"Which of you by being anxious is able to add even a single hour to your life?

32"All these things are what the Gentiles prioritize, and your Heavenly Father knows that you need them all. 33Prioritize first the kingdom of God and his righteousness instead, and all these things will be added to you."

Matthew 6:25, 27, 32-33 AT

Chapter 3 | Reality Check

How do you decide where your time gets spent? Chances are a large amount is decided for you by work and family commitments. But how about the rest? How much of your time is yours to direct where you choose?

Most people are in an unhealthy relationship with time. The visible commodities we deal in might be money, goods and services, but the one commodity that we are constantly using up is measured by the clock. Your life has been expiring one second at a time since you started breathing, and it will continue to do so until you stop.

Scary thought?

It's just part of being human.

Time is our most precious resource, and the one which we cannot stash away or put in an account to earn interest or invest to pay us dividends. And it's not lost on me that you are choosing to spend it reading this, so I will make it worth your while.

Before the arrival of certain technologies, humans were forced to comply with the limitations of time. We would wake up with the sun and stop work when it could no longer be done.

But since we started measuring time mechanically rather than by nature, we have been able to break free from the created order of time and establish our own rhythm. Fast forward to the invention of the light bulb, and now we can work or play at any time of day or night.

Those poor, *unenlightened* people before Edison's invention in 1879 were forced to cease being productive at dusk and instead, spent those wasted nights getting an average of 11 hours of sleep.[15] Oh, how we pity them...

But this progress in technology has fed the insatiable efficiency-monster of modern life. We are in a frantic quest to squeeze every possible outcome out of our limited time. The more efficient we can be, the further we will get in life. It's our raging defiance against the relentless limitation of time.

It's also our attempt to do everything, be everywhere, and to quench the terrible Fear Of Missing Out. Those cultural narratives appear most frequently through our priorities, and shout loudest through our fears. And it's those two things, our priorities and our fears, which dictate how we spend our time.

Jesus' view of time is far more grounded than ours:

> *"Which of you by being anxious is able to add even a single hour to your life?"*

---

[15] Arwen Curry, "How Electric Light Changed the Night," KQED, January 20, 2015, www.kqed.org/science/26331/how-electric-light-changed-the-night

Chapter 3 | Reality Check

This passage is speaking about God's desire and ability to provide. It's speaking to the fears which inform how we spend our time. But most importantly, it is teaching us that there is a way to overcome the fears of missing out, not having enough, or of failing at life, which does not succumb to anxiety. Finding a life ruled by the presence of God rather than anxiety and fear is a good description of Soul Rest.

There is clear comfort in these verses from Matthew. We shouldn't worry about our lives because God cares for us, and he wants to provide for our needs. We are more precious to him than the birds, who receive his care and attention, so why would he not meet our needs?

But we cannot take the comfort from these verses if we don't also take the instruction: seek first the kingdom of God.

Jesus draws a clear line between those who know how to seek the kingdom and those who don't. The group who don't are called 'gentiles', which is simply the first century Jewish term for a non-Jew. The gentiles form their priorities by the cultural narratives around them, rather than by the one who created their soul. The same could be said about any of us who let our cultural narratives form our priorities instead of God.

It's our priorities which then dictate how we spend our time. So, if we want to know whether someone is seeking the kingdom of God, the evidence is in how they spend their time.

What does your schedule say about what's important to you?

What does it look like to have correctly ordered priorities? It may strike you that everything Jesus is asking us to slide down the priority list is critical to basic survival. How long would you survive without food, water, shelter or clothing?

He's not targeting worldly indulgences like restaurant meals, long holidays, larger and flatter TVs, or tickets to the Australian Open. He speaks about the absolute basics of human existence, the things which keep us alive.

If the way to be freed from a life ruled by fear and anxiety is to prioritise the kingdom of God over even the bare necessities of life, how much more should all the other pursuits in our life give way?

Don't forget, the pursuit comes with a promise. When your priorities, including the way you spend your time, are in order, God himself will meet your needs. You are a being of dust and breath. When you prioritise the breath-needs, God meets the dust-needs. That's always been his design.

It should go without saying that this doesn't mean abandoning your job and relying on welfare so you can meditate 24/7. It's about priorities, and what I am trying to prove to you is that it is about *time*.

Jesus is asking for your time.

The habits and practices which feed your soul (spiritual disciplines) all require time. Receiving the flow of life from God to our souls happens at the same speed as the rest of our life: one second at a time. You cannot abide in the vine without spending your time with Him.

I have found myself guilty of uttering a common but nonsensical request: *I wish there were more hours in the day*. I get frustrated when a task takes longer than I anticipate. But the concept of being given more time is absurd. The one thing we cannot get is more time.

There will always and forever be 24 hours in a day. You will always and forever need to spend some of that time eating, sleeping and taking care of your body. And you will always and forever need to spend some of that time connecting with God, fulfilling the purpose for which you were made.

We have it backwards. We don't need more time. We need to do less stuff.

Do you have time to connect with God?

Prayer for today

Dear God, thank you that you made the world with natural limits. Show me where my life tries to go over these limits and help me to see its effect on me. Help me to order my priorities in the way you have designed.

Amen.

Chapter 3 | Reality Check

3.3
Admitting Defeat

But [Jesus] would withdraw to desolate places to pray.

Luke 5:16

Admitting defeat is liberating. The moment we learn to accept the limitations of time, we shed the burdens of achieving the impossible. The burdens of doing everything and being everything. The burden of living up to unnecessary expectations. Accepting our limitations exposes our self-inflicted pressures as unrealistic: *incompatible with reality*. Why would we let them cause us so much worry?

So far, we have been on a journey of detox. We have identified what our soul is and what is making it sick, and I hope last week's readings have prompted you to uproot some negative factors in your inward life. But the reason many of us never find Soul Rest is because we stop at that first step. We stop there because the second step seems unnecessary without a good reality check.

First, we started clearing the weeds. Now we are feeding the plant.

When it boils down, the only tool we have to feed the plant is time. It doesn't matter what spiritual discipline we are engaged in, we pay for them with the same currency: time.

Frighteningly, we are the most time-poor people in history.

Are you seeing now the connection between a busy, hurried life, and poor soul health? Not only is the pace of life rewiring our brains and harming our souls, but it is starving our very ability to fix the problem. It's a double-edged sword.

The next step has to be clear now. It's highly likely you will need to create time in your life—not by somehow defying physics, but by letting something else go. Not because it's bad, but because it's competing with your ability to feed your soul. Remember, time is your most limited and precious resource.

When Jesus said to 'come to him' so that he might 'give us rest', he wasn't talking about a transaction where we walk away fixed. He was talking about a pursuit of him. And when he said to 'take his yoke', he was, in part, inviting us to mimic his life.

He alone, as the expert on our souls, was able to live this life perfectly.

Yes, Jesus' perfection meant he never sinned like us. But it also meant that he lived his life the way we should live it, not just in his moral example, but in how he spent his time. So, it stands to reason that when we see Jesus doing something, we should do it.

Anyone remember those bracelets? WWJD: What Would Jesus Do? It turns out, Luke 5:16 tells us exactly what he would do. He would often withdraw to pray. It wasn't an isolated incident; it was his habit, his sustaining rhythm.

Many groups historically have discovered the life-giving power of regular prayer. One such group is the monastic movement which started in the fourth century, and with various ebbs and flows, continues today.

Monastic life was (and is) simple and revolves around two things: work and prayer. Its view is that these two things are the fundamental rhythms of the created order, to pursue God's face, and to work the earth.[16] Dust and breath.

It is impossible to overstate the importance of prayer in monastic life. Every activity is punctuated by prayer. It's the

---

[16] Sittser, G. *Water from a Deep Well.* 2007. pp 97

first task in the morning and the last at night. It would be done as monks transition from one task to another. There are rote prayers, contemplative prayers, and spontaneous prayers. Their lives revolve around the rhythm of prayer.

This seems extreme. Is there anything so worthwhile that we would pick it up at every spare moment, between every task, and at the bookends of our day?

Oh wait—it's in your pocket.

Why would someone choose to depart normal life and submit to the crippling rhythm of a monastic rule? In addition to the constant prayer, monks would only gain entry to the order after taking some variation of a vow of poverty, celibacy and consecration. They would promise to always be poor, single, and boring. Any takers?

But the monks discovered something that we don't know. Now more than ever, we need their wisdom. Gerald Sittser writes on monastic life from both academic rigour and deep personal experience with the benefits of monastic rhythm:

"Monasteries sanctify time, as if to show that all time belongs to God and our use of time finds meaning only if we do our tasks, both religious and secular, to honor and serve God."[17]

---

[17] Ibid.

Giving our time to God means giving some things up. It means choosing to let go of habits or pursuits which may be good, simply because life is too full to give God the time he deserves, and that our souls need. That is baldly opposed to the narrative that you can have it all, achieve it all, do it all. No, you can't. You must make a choice.

It's fitting to revisit Jesus' words here:

> [26] *For what will it benefit you if you gain the whole world but your soul is given away? What can you give in exchange for your soul?*
>
> *Matthew 16:26 AT*

Jesus isn't demanding that you shave your head and only own one set of clothes (but hey, if the simplicity of a single t-shirt is appealing, don't let me stop you). But he could be suggesting that you pare back your time on Netflix, or reduce your extra-curriculars, or delete your Instagram account, or even that you say no to extra work. Not because you're obliged to, but because your soul needs that time with God.

Perhaps the most important decision in your spiritual life is not the evil you resist, but what good you choose to lay down in offering to God.

It's all down to your priorities. Will you let God determine them? When everything you spend your time on—good, bad or neutral—is weighed against your soul, which one are you willing to give up?

Prayer for today

Dear God, show me how I can make room in my life. Help me to reorder my priorities to begin feeding my soul. Give me the courage to make the choices that need to be made.

Amen.

Soul Rest

3.4
Weekly reflection

Write down all the things in your life which take regular bites of your schedule, whether good, bad, or neutral and split them into these two columns:

Essential	Non-essential
_____	_____
_____	_____
_____	_____
_____	_____
_____	_____
_____	_____

Essential	Non-essential
_____	_____
_____	_____
_____	_____
_____	_____
_____	_____

How much room is there in your schedule to connect with God through a spiritual discipline?

_____

_____

_____

_____

_____

_____

_____

Soul Rest

If you already have spiritual disciplines in place, how adequately do you feel they are feeding your soul?

_____

_____

_____

_____

_____

_____

_____

_____

_____

_____

_____

_____

_____

_____

Chapter 3 | Reality Check

What is one thing you could pare back, reprioritize, or remove altogether from your life to replace with a spiritual discipline?

_____
_____
_____
_____
_____
_____
_____

How would it look to act on it for the rest of the course?

_____
_____
_____
_____
_____
_____
_____

3.5

Group Session

This week has been all about making time in our lives and recognizing our limitations. It is about accepting reality. We are each a finite resource and life is full of competing priorities all vying for our schedules. If soul health is a priority for us, it must be reflected in how we spend our time.

DISCUSSION QUESTIONS

1. What did you think of this week's readings?

2. What stood out to you the most?

Chapter 3 | Reality Check

3. Share your schedule with the group and ask: what would you say are the visible priorities in my life, given where my time is spent?

4. Reflect on the people who have had significant influence in your life (parents, family, friends, etc.). What kind of example did they set with their time and how has it influenced you?

How often do you find yourself saying something like, 'I would love to ____ but I just don't have the time right now'? A common experience of time in our context is one of helplessness and futility. The season of motherhood is particularly difficult in this regard. Often looking after our own needs goes out the window when we give everything to those who are dependent on us.

In seasons like this when factoring soul health into our own schedules seems impossible, there are two avenues open to us:

    1. Recalibrate our priorities and our capacity

Usually, something can give. Most people write things in their 'essential' column which can be moved if their sense of priority and their own limitation are adjusted. Soul health is either important enough to make the list, or it isn't.

    2. Find a way to connect to God alongside our duties

If truly nothing at all can change about our schedule and capacity, God understands that. He doesn't want to leave us high and dry just because we are a mother, or an on-call worker, or trapped in circumstances beyond our control. We are still able, as difficult as it may be, to connect with God in our heart and mind alongside the inescapable elements of our schedule.

5. Which one of these options best describes your schedule?

6. What have you chosen to reduce or remove in your life to create room to connect with God?

Pray for each other:

- To figure out how to make room for God and to follow through
- To feel a greater sense of God's presence alongside daily activity

Chapter 3 | Reality Check

Soul Rest

CHAPTER 4
Paradox

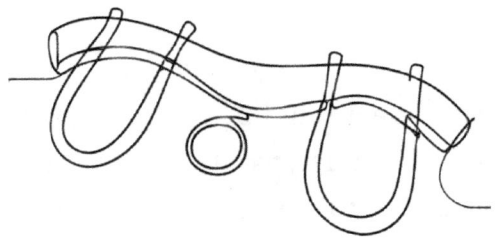

4.1

Jesus' Yoke

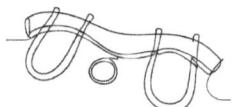

"Take my yoke upon you, and learn from me, for I am gentle and lowly in heart, and you will find rest for your souls. For my yoke is easy, and my burden is light."

Matthew 11:29-30

Picture a modern Queensland beach. The sun sparkles on the rich blue water as a lonely container ship glides along the distant horizon. Closer to the shore but still a way out, surfers paddle along waiting for the perfect wave. The squeals of children ride the sea breeze as everyone attempts to squint through the harsh glare. The beach is dotted with cabanas and sunburnt backs.

But one other feature has come to dominate the beach landscape of modern Queensland: the humble pull-along wagon. Although my wife suggested one for years, some deep anti-conforming pride stopped me from caving. But ever since we bought one, I have not stopped singing its praises. The best part—not only do I not have to carry all our beach gear across the sand, but getting three little children off the beach is no longer a half-hour saga of burning feet and tired legs. The wagon does the work, so I don't have to.

A yoke is a piece of equipment we aren't very familiar with in our day and age. It took many forms, but its simplest was a wooden beam that would rest on the back of a bull, ox, donkey, or other beast of burden, and connect it to a piece of farming equipment—usually something to plough the dirt. The yoke was a way to harness the strength of the animal and set it to a desired task. Just like my wagon, it did the work, so the farmer didn't have to.

For the agricultural society that Jesus lived in, the imagery of the yoke would have been very accessible. Perhaps there was even a nearby field with a yoked beast that the crowd could stare at in contemplation.

Perhaps they saw two bulls joined by a yoke at the shoulders, one young bull yet to submit to its yoke, and one old bull that had ploughed his field for years. They watched as the young bull tossed its head, attempting to throw off the yoke, kicking pointlessly against the frame. Perhaps they noticed the rippling strength of the old bull, unmoved by the young bull's antics, steady and determined in ploughing his field, one row at a time. His impressive strength evoked awe.

But perhaps some of the crowd took offense. Why is Jesus comparing me to a farm animal? Analogy or not, I have my dignity. And if he is really trying to promise rest and relief from burdens, why is he suggesting taking on a piece of farming equipment?

These are valid questions which show the paradox in what Jesus said. His invitation is to those who are already burdened and heavy laden. His invitation is to those who need rest. Surely, the last thing these people need is a burden of a different kind. Shouldering an apparatus that is designed for work sounds like the opposite of rest.

And then there's the awkward reality that taking on a yoke requires *submission*. This Soul Rest thing is beginning to sound like a bait-and-switch.

That is, until we realise that every single one of us is already under a yoke.

In fact, we are likely under many different yokes. Perhaps you have felt the weight of them:

- The yoke of performance and success. I can't fail.
- The yoke of productivity. I need to be making things happen and not waste time.

- The yoke of fitting in. It's an immense burden to make sure I'm dressing right, speaking right, acting right, buying the right things, attending the right events, all to get other people to like me.
- The yoke of self-expectation. I don't care what others think but I hold myself to high standards, and I can't let them slip.
- The yoke of improvement. I must create a better life for my kids than the one I received from my parents.
- The yoke of addiction. As much as I would like to stop, I can't.

The list goes on. Somewhere along the way, we conclude that life is about minimizing burdens. We work hard, get a good education and research every decision ultimately so that we can lessen these burdens.

It's why our society is so obsessed with escapist behaviours: the alternate reality of video gaming or porn; the altered reality of abusing alcohol or drugs; the escape of scrolling media. While not all these things are innately wrong, unhealthy use of anything like these makes it a yoke.

Frederick Dale Bruner, theologian and author, puts it this way:

"Realism sees that life is a succession of burdens; we cannot get away from them; thus instead of offering escape, Jesus offers equipment."

Bruner highlights that it's not only destructive behaviours that create for us a yoke. It's just life. Jesus does not present the false hope of escaping life's burdens. That's why what he offers is a trade. Your burdens for his.

And his burdens?

Light and easy.

Not the meal prep company—the yoke of Jesus.

It's the reason that taking on his yoke makes sense. There's no bait-and-switch. What you are shedding is the immense weight of life which you were not meant to bear on your own. What you are receiving is the borrowed strength of the one who was able to live life the way it was meant to be lived.

When you take on Jesus' yoke, you are freed from the mastery of those other burdens of life. The truth of the picture is that Jesus is the old bull already under the yoke. He's ploughed the field before us, and his strength is all that is required. He could do it on his own, but the yoke is designed to train the younger bull. That's us.

It's only when the younger bull submits to the yoke and to the strength of the old bull that he realizes the yoke is easy. Not because the task is easy, but because the old bull is doing all the work. His broad shoulders are bearing the weight, and his powerful legs are breaking the ground. All we have to do is walk alongside him and learn to turn when he turns and go where he goes.

This is the same as abiding in the vine. It's the same as pursuing Jesus. To find rest for our souls, we must learn to live a life that is constantly and consciously aware of Jesus, both the comforting presence of his strength beside us, and the direction of his life. The closer we can walk with him, the easier our yoke will be.

Prayer for today

Thank you, Jesus, that you have offered me your easy yoke. Help me to learn what it means to step under it beside you and walk with you. Would you help me to feel your comforting presence right now and throughout the day. Help me to remember you in all that I do and feel your rest today.

Amen.

4.2
Working from Rest

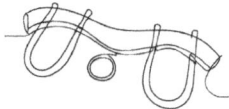

"Take my yoke upon you, and learn from me, for I am gentle and lowly in heart…"

Matthew 11:29

Transport your mind back to our last reading and the picture of the bulls in the field. We're three and a half weeks into a six-week journey to finding Soul Rest. I wonder if you expected rest to look like heavy, rudimentary farm work?

I was kind of hoping Soul Rest looked like the destination videos they show you on the plane before landing.

I'm sure the irony wasn't lost on the people listening to Jesus. Rest sure didn't look like accepting a yoke. But Jesus isn't just being ironic here. There is a real sense in which his yoke is both work and rest. It's a paradox.

There is a great temptation in pursuing Jesus' Soul Rest, and that is to believe that we can get from Jesus what we always sought through following cultural narratives: an easy, relaxing life with no responsibility, plenty of spare time, and maybe even a little luxury. If that's what you're buying, Jesus isn't selling.

Twice in my life when playing soccer, I've torn an Anterior Cruciate Ligament in my knee—a matching set. It's a common injury but usually requires surgery to fix. My physique has always resembled spaghetti strands hanging off a fork, but even I was shocked at how quickly after surgery my quads atrophied from sturdy bamboo to limp noodle. I lost sixteen straight seasons of physical conditioning in two weeks of immobilisation.

And the other side effect? Uncharacteristic depression.

The problem with pursuing ease is *atrophy*. When our bodies don't move, they start to die, and our souls are the same. Pulling back on commitments, creating more spare time, and listening to the natural limitations of our body and soul are necessary. So is finding a healthy and sustainable rhythm of work and rest. But it shouldn't lead to laziness. A lazy soul is a selfish soul.

Soul Rest isn't only about adopting better prayer rhythms and being continually mindful of Jesus' presence throughout the day. A healthy soul leads an active life from the place of rest.

The paradox here is found in the fact that when you take on Jesus' yoke, it's God's strength that enables you to live life.

Exactly what kind of life, though? The kind that *learns from him*; the kind that is *gentle and lowly*.

One person who exemplified Jesus' easy yoke was the Apostle Paul. But his life did not look easy. He was frequently imprisoned, beaten, ostracised, and almost stoned to death.[18] In Ephesus, he worked as a tanner in the mornings before delivering public lectures for five hours, daily. For two years.[19] He travelled countries on foot, sailed the seas, surviving a few shipwrecks, and through all this he was a prolific author.

Paul reflects on his 'easy yoke' like this:

> *"For this I toil, struggling with all his energy that he powerfully works within me."*
>
> *Colossians 1:29*

---

[18] 2 Corinthians 11:23-28
[19] In Acts 19:9-10, Paul moves from preaching in the Jewish synagogue in Ephesus to the public hall of Tyrannus, delivering lectures daily. The Western Text adds that he preached from 11am to 4pm.

Chapter 4 | Paradox

This is the paradox of the easy yoke. Paul lived a life that accomplished far more than we could hope to achieve. It was a life that didn't look easy. He may have even been accused of overdoing it, working too hard and resting too little. But for Paul, this was the easiest life he could live.

Why?

Borrowed strength.

Literally, God's energy.

But here's the honest catch. Paul wasn't toiling for his own desires anymore. He hadn't transferred his hopes of a plump superannuation, ocean view and lucrative book royalties to *Jesus Super inc.* His desires were forever formed by the one whose yoke he had taken.

That's the thing about a yoke—it makes going your own way *harder*. Even *impossible*.

Accepting the yoke of Jesus is not about asking him to grant your wishes. God will not empower the life you want to live. He will not lend his strength for your agenda. Accepting his yoke means you accept that his way is The Way.

Can such an offer be trusted? Can I really give up the way I thought life should be lived and trust that Jesus has something better? This offer seems in some ways, harsh and arrogant.

That's exactly why Jesus reassures us it's quite the opposite:

> "...for I am **gentle** and **lowly** in heart, and you will find rest for your souls."

Jesus went to great lengths to prove his trustworthiness in this deal, the extent of which we will explore next week. Giving up our yokes for his requires the trust that he truly is gentle and lowly.

Prayer for today

Dear God, help me to understand what it means to take your yoke. Help me to take stock of the cost. Help me to trust that this offer of rest comes from a gentle and lowly heart. Help me have the gentle and lowly heart required to receive it. Show me if there are parts of my life that don't fit with your yoke.

Amen.

Chapter 4 | Paradox

4.3

The Place of Rest

"Do not store up for yourselves treasures on earth, where moths and vermin destroy, and where thieves break in and steal. [20] But store up for yourselves treasures in heaven, where moths and vermin do not destroy, and where thieves do not break in and steal. [21] For where your treasure is, there your heart will be also."

Matthew 6:19-21 NIV

We've been talking about the multi-layered paradox in Jesus' yoke. Firstly, true rest is found in submitting to equipment, not in escaping the burdens of life. Secondly, a rested soul doesn't look like an inactive one. Jesus was very active in his life and constantly gave of his time. He allowed himself to be continually interrupted by the needs of others, never so busy or consumed in his own task to ignore the delightful children, desperate parents, or diseased outcasts who sought him.

These paradoxes mean that finding Soul Rest involves elements you may not have anticipated. It means living a life full of purpose. It's a life that satisfies the parts of our soul which need meaning and productivity. It's a life that can endure the many trials and burdens we inevitably face. It's abundant and full life.

How is it, exactly, that Jesus' yoke enables us to live this kind of life? The answer is the same as the catch cry of the real estate world:

It's all about location, location, location.

The words of Matthew 6 for today appear in the same context as last week's reading. When Jesus instructs us not to be anxious and to accept the limitations of our finite life, these words about treasure are part of the solution.

Our deep restlessness is the result of toiling to satisfy a soul built for eternity with things that will fade. Of course, we need to eat, drink, and be clothed, but if our hearts are set on those pursuits, something deep inside our subconscious is still afraid for eternity, because unlike God, these things will eventually fade.

If our lives are set up to pursue wealth, achievements, status, friendships, significance, luxury, leisure, or any other number of shiny objects—even if we are wildly successful in that pursuit—our subconscious souls will still ache for eternal security. Deep down in every soul is the knowledge that our pursuits have a limit, but our soul is made to last.

The ancient king and philosopher of Israel, Solomon, put it this way:

> *"He has made everything beautiful in its time. He has also set eternity in the human heart; yet no one can fathom what God has done from beginning to end."*
>
> *Ecclesiastes 3:11*

The dust and breath tension is beautifully visible in this thought. Everything we see is beautiful in its time. The beauty of a flower is in the fact that it fades. Actually, its beauty is only borrowed temporarily from the one who imagined its existence and gave it life. The pleasures and wonders of the finite world are to be appreciated within their seasons in full knowledge that they are temporary pointers to the majesty of an eternal God.

These observations are in tension with the fact that deep within us, our souls long for eternity. They long for the one who gave the flower beauty more than they long for the flower itself. The most important elements of life which flow out of the cravings of our souls—meaning, purpose, connection, vitality—will only lead us to rest when they are set in the right *place*.

Jesus' words then show us where they are to be set. While he talks mostly about our treasure, his real concern is for our heart. He expresses it backwards because he knows that if we place our treasures in the eternal sphere (heaven) rather than the temporary sphere (earth), our heart will follow.

This eternal security is what calms our restless souls. When we know that our treasure and our heart is placed in heaven, the cravings of our souls which God designed to be with him forever finally find their peace.

How do we do it?

The same way we handle our physical treasure. If I want to move my savings from a stagnant, interest-earning account to a highly-geared investment that will pay off well in the future, the first thing I need to do is make a withdrawal. I take my treasure out of its current place, and deposit it elsewhere.

So, think for a moment: what are the true cravings of your soul? It may take asking a few 'why' questions to dig down to the deepest layer.

My soul longs to... succeed in my job.

Why?

Because I want to be seen as valuable to my boss, my family and society.

Why?

Because I need to be valued by someone I find significant.

And that's the treasure. So, who is the significant person? My boss, spouse, or society? Then I consciously withdraw that treasure from their hands and put it in God's.

Make sense?

So, what is your treasure?

The desire to be wanted, loved? The desire to lead a meaningful life? The desire to help and grow your own children, or help people? The desire to be a good person? The desire to accept and love yourself? The desire to know who you really are? The desire to be whole and not broken? To be healthy and not sick?

My soul longs to...

_____

_____

_____

Chapter 4 | Paradox

_____

_____

_____

Now think about where this treasure is currently placed. In your job success? In your family success or stability? In the acceptance of a parent or mentor or loved one? In the amount of your savings or investments or your business's bottom line? In the recognition of others?

My treasure is currently placed in:

_____

_____

_____

_____

_____

_____

_____

Now make a conscious withdrawal. Imagine yourself approaching that 'place' in your mind and withdrawing your life savings from that person or idea. Reduce your balance to zero and close the account.

Now take those life savings and bring them to God.

Pray

God, I offer you these deep longings of my soul because they are made for you. I deposit them into your trust which is eternally secure in heaven. I ask you to keep them there for eternity and I trust that they are safe with you, and I will never be disappointed by them.

Amen.

Now there are two important realities you need to know if you have successfully made the withdrawal and deposit.

Firstly, the place of your treasure and subsequently your heart also becomes your place of rest. There is a peace which your soul feels in finally answering its eternal desire in an eternal God. But the wonderful reality is that God allows that rest to flow from eternity into our souls right here and now. That peace and rest sustains us in this difficult life.

Secondly, this is an ongoing process. We tend to revert to investing in worldly places as the complexity of life grows with us. You may need to make this withdrawal on a regular basis and reset your hope in eternity. Keep transferring your treasure to God.

Read what he says in his word about those deep longings of your soul. Trust his answers and his promises. Rest in him.

4.4

Weekly Reflection

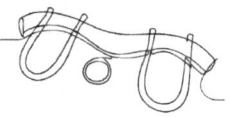

What yokes am I under in my life? These could be practical yokes, or anything that weighs down my soul.

_____

_____

_____

_____

_____

_____

_____

_____

When we reflect honestly on these yokes, sometimes we place ourselves under them. Some people struggle to say 'no' to things. We can all make choices which bring us under heavy burdens. Are there any of these burdens I have put upon myself? If so, how?

Soul Rest

Which yokes are forced upon me?

_____

_____

_____

_____

_____

_____

How might moving the place of my desires (reading 3) affect my experience of these yokes?

_____

_____

_____

_____

_____

_____

Chapter 4 | Paradox

Which of these yokes or cravings of the soul do I still need answers for? Am I left with any big questions?

_____
_____
_____
_____
_____
_____
_____
_____
_____
_____
_____
_____
_____
_____

4.5 Group Session

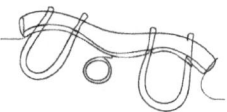

This week we have been discussing the paradox of Jesus' yoke. Rather than offering escape from the burdens of life, Jesus offers us equipment to endure them. Rather than inviting us to a life of empty leisure, he invites us to a purposeful, active and influential life, working under his yoke alongside him.

Taking Jesus' yoke upon us doesn't just mean giving up our old way of life which was never working for us; it means giving over our whole life to God. His hands are the safe place where we can deposit our treasure and trust. The great secret of an energised and meaningful life under Jesus' yoke is to learn to trust him to do the hard work. We work with his divine energy.

DISCUSSION QUESTIONS

1. What did you think of the readings this week?

2. What stood out to you the most?

3. How did you answer the questions about the yokes in your life?

4. Did you do the 'withdrawal and deposit' exercise? How did it go?

Sometimes there are areas of our lives which we would like to give over to God, but for some reason it never seems to work. There might be a persistent addiction we can't shake, or a trauma we can't forgive. It's possible that by digging down a few layers below the immediate situation, we find that there is a treasure, a deep need of our soul, which is deposited in the wrong place.

5. Are there any areas in your life you have struggled to fully hand over to God?

6. Did this week leave you with any deeper questions you would like to bring to the group?

Pray for each other:

- To be freed from yokes
- To successfully shift treasure from places that will always disappoint into God's safe hands
- To continue to have victory in detoxing

Chapter 4 | Paradox

Soul Rest

CHAPTER 5

The Yoke of the Cross

5.1

An Uncomfortable Question

Pilate said to them, "Then what shall I do with Jesus who is called Christ?" They all said, "Let him be crucified!" [23] And he said, "Why? What evil has he done?" But they shouted all the more, "Let him be crucified!"

Matthew 27:22-23

A crowd is gathered in a large, open courtyard in the centre of the city of ancient Jerusalem. The outline of the stone palace glows gold as the sun attempts to rise over the parapets. In the shadowed courtyard, angry Jews with their pious chins lifted toward the Roman official's platform shout at Pontius Pilate, as he struggles to comprehend their request.

Chapter 5 | The Yoke of the Cross

Next to him on the platform stands a man with the strong shoulders of a tradesman and a steely gaze, unmoved but somehow tinted with compassion. In three hours' time, the man would be hanging on a rough wooden cross, mostly naked, suspended in the air by iron nails the size of railroad spikes mercilessly driven through his wrists and feet. He would be unrecognisable. Beaten, flailed, bloodied and in clinical shock.

Pilate at this moment asks an awkward but pertinent question:

Why?

In the mob-adrenaline-fuelled, hell-for-leather highway chase of Jesus' arrest and trial, that question could barely apply the brakes. The crowd smelled blood.

Why should Jesus be crucified?

It's a question that warrants explanation now 2,000 years later just as much as it did in that moment, though perhaps historical perspective gives us an advantage over the furious mob. The answer is bound up in another 'why' question that we have not yet paused to ask over this course.

Why do we need Soul Rest?

Why are you reading this book? Wasn't your life perfectly fine five weeks ago? Or might there be a universally-felt

135

restlessness of the soul for which all humanity is desperate to find the solution?

Jesus' answer: because we are burdened and heavy laden.

And where did the burdens come from?

We've explored a great deal of why modern life makes the situation worse. Factors both internally and externally leave us burdened. But the spiritual problem came much earlier.

The gentle way to put it is that we've misunderstood the nature and purpose of our souls' existence. We were created to be connected to God, experiencing him as our source of life by living the way he designed us.

The clinical assessment is not so gentle. Every single one of us by nature and choice has rejected that design. We've proverbially flipped God the bird and taken charge of our own lives. We know best and our way to run both the earth and our own broken lives must be better than the primary being in the universe.

In short, we were created to *need God,* but we desired to *be God.*

Chapter 5 | The Yoke of the Cross

The result is disconnection from the being who made life and sustains it by his will.[20] We cut the cords of our own parachute and have been feeling the soul-deep restlessness of freefall ever since.

Can it be reversed?

Yes, which is the real reason you're here. So, how?

Now we're answering Pilate's question.

Jesus looks out upon the crowd of angry faces. He sees wrath. He sees a level of fury only achieved by religious indignance. He understands his fate. The night before, he wrestled agonisingly with God in prayer. The wrestle to bend God's design away from his painful death had failed, but the wrestle to submit every quaking cell of his body to this courageous sacrifice had succeeded.

Flashes of conversations run through his mind. He spots a man hiding in the shadowy colonnades beside the crowd, an ornate prayer shawl drawn to obscure his identity. He recalls a late-night, secret conversation with this man:

---

[20] Hebrews 1:3

> *"For God so loved the world that he gave his only son, so that whoever believes in him will not perish, but have eternal life."*
>
> *John 3:16*

Jesus knew Nicodemus, the Pharisee with the drawn shawl, was thinking of that same conversation. And at this moment, Nicodemus was realising what Jesus meant by the word 'gave'. The Son of God was not just given *to* mankind; he was *given over* to mankind to be killed. God didn't just give his Son; he *gave up* his Son.

Jesus reminds himself of his Father's motive. Love. And as his eye's meet Nicodemus' hidden in the crowd, the reason why Jesus needed to be crucified becomes clear.

The angry mob.

Who will love them? Who will save them from their self-righteous rejection of God's way? Who could show them that God's love runs deeper than their hatred? Who could prove without a shadow of a doubt that God's love would go to the very end to win them back from their spiritual freefall? Who would be gentle and lowly enough?

They won't listen. They won't be reasoned with. They're blinded by their need to run their own lives. Nicodemus looks at the crowd and realises that Jesus in that very moment by his silence is showing them the love they don't deserve but so desperately need.

The angry mob is us. We've chosen to be the masters of our own lives, and we would rather drown out the awkward question, 'why?', with the shouts of autocracy.

Jesus died because we needed him to.

We needed his sacrifice to atone for our sins, and we needed his courage and strength to endure the slings and arrows of our spiritual blindness. We needed to trade our brokenness for his wholeness, an outrageously unfair exchange, but the spiritual defibrillation we desperately required.

Jesus died to prove God's love to us. Because he did not spare himself, we are able to trust him with this exchange. Our souls are safe in his hands.

Prayer for today

Dear God, I thank you that Jesus died for me. I thank you that he saw my needs and chose to meet them at his own expense. I thank you that he demonstrated his love and earned my trust in making the ultimate sacrifice. I entrust my soul to you. I admit that I need you and I let go of the desire to be the god of my own life.

Amen.

5.2

A Cross for a Yoke

So they took Jesus, ¹⁷ and he went out, bearing his own cross, to the place called The Place of a Skull, which in Aramaic is called Golgotha. ¹⁸ There they crucified him, and with him two others, one on either side, and Jesus between them.

John 19:16b-18

The most important parts of a narrative are told as if they are in slow motion. Most of my year 9 English students were more interested in hiding their Minecraft game in a separate window than heeding my writing advice, but it worked for those who listened.

That's not just a narrative technique, though; it's how our brains work. When we want to communicate something

Chapter 5 | The Yoke of the Cross

important, we slow down, use clear and descriptive language, and ensure the impact of the point is driven home.

The four gospels, Matthew, Mark, Luke, and John, tell the history of Jesus' life, focussing on the three years from the beginning of his public ministry until his death.[21] Of those three years, each writer focuses between 30-50% of their work on Jesus' final seven days.[22]

These are the days of his entry into Jerusalem, rising conflict with the religious leaders, his farewell discourse with his disciples, the last supper, his arrest, trial, crucifixion, and resurrection.

The gospel writers want us to understand the significance of this final week of Jesus' life. They compel us: *don't attempt to understand Jesus without the cross*. Every memorable teaching of his ministry finds greater illumination with the light of the cross shed upon it.

To understand Jesus' yoke and his invitation to Soul Rest in Matthew 11, it is essential that we examine the cross of John 19. In fact, the two moments share profound similarity. In the first, Jesus prompts the people to picture him under the heavy

---

[21] Matthew and Luke record Jesus' birth, John gives a philosophical prologue, and Mark launches straight into the action at his baptism.
[22] Matthew, Mark and Luke are at about a third each, and John gives almost half his work to this final week.

burden of a wooden beam, hard at work, sweat dripping from his face in the beating sun.

In the second, there is no need to imagine.

Jesus carried his cross. [23] The people saw the drops of sweat mixed with blood. He ploughed not a field, but a path to his sacrifice. Just like the yoke, that heavy beam of wood symbolised his work, but instead of working the earth, he was doing the work of a saviour.

We must understand Jesus' cross to understand his invitation to rest, because the cross was his work. What he promised through the words, 'I will give you rest', he proved at the cross. He proved his strength, he proved his character, and he proved his heart for us.

Remarkably, the arrest, trial and crucifixion of Jesus was recorded by a fifth biblical author 700 years before it happened. The prophet Isaiah speaks with uncanny specificity about Jesus' death.

---

[23] The three synoptic gospels (Matthew, Mark and Luke) all include the detail that a man named Simon of Cyrene was compelled to carry Jesus' cross for him (Mt 27:32, Mk 15:21, Lk 23:26). As an eyewitness to the events and traditionally the last to write his account, John is not making a mistake here but wanting to highlight a different detail. For at least part of the journey, Jesus carried his own cross.

Chapter 5 | The Yoke of the Cross

> *He was oppressed and afflicted, yet he did not open his mouth;*
> *he was led like a lamb to the slaughter,*
> *and as a sheep before its shearers is silent,*
> *so he did not open his mouth.*
>
> *Isaiah 53:7*

Jesus is often given the title in the New Testament, 'The Lamb of God', in recognition of both his sacrifice and his character. These verses drip with prophetic significance. Jesus went to the cross on the very weekend the Passover was celebrated—the ritual which symbolised the death of a lamb as a substitute for the people of Israel. The picture also ratifies Jesus' claims of being 'gentle and lowly of heart.'

Isaiah's passage not only confirms Jesus' death as pre-planned according to God's design, but it provides an interpretation of its significance:

> *Surely he took up our pain and bore our suffering...*
> *⁵ But he was pierced for our transgressions,*
> *he was crushed for our iniquities;*
> *the punishment that brought us peace was on him,*
> *and by his wounds we are healed.*
> *⁶ We all, like sheep, have gone astray,*
> *each of us has turned to our own way;*
> *and the Lord has laid on him the iniquity of us all.*
>
> *Isaiah 53:4-6*

Soul Rest

Isaiah interprets the cross for us. The burden that Jesus bore on the cross was our pain, our suffering. The punctures he endured were for our transgressions, the crushing for our wrongdoing. The yoke Jesus bore was ours.

Suddenly, his promise in Matthew 11 becomes clear. Are you burdened and heavy laden? Jesus knows that you are. He sees the weight of your iniquity. And on the cross he felt it. He carried it. "Come to me," he says, "and I will give you rest."

We finally find rest in Jesus because he took our burdens upon himself on the cross. He lifted them off our shoulders and they sank down on his, adding to the weight upon his nail-pierced hands. This is the unique and unparalleled claim of Jesus. No other religion or historical figure dares to wipe away our burdens by their own sacrifice.

"Take my yoke upon you"

He is offering us an exchange. 'Give me your heavy, burdened life,' he says. 'You aren't able to bear it, but I am. Lay down the pressure of being your own master, and instead, take my yoke. It's light. It is the one perfect, spotless, weightless life.'

"For I am gentle and lowly in heart"

Chapter 5 | The Yoke of the Cross

Jesus pleads with us, 'I have accepted my fate with a meekness and strength that only a divine, loving God could. Let that be the proof to you. If I can carry the sins of the world with such compassion and tenderness, what do you have to fear?'

"You will find rest for your souls."

Far more than a self-help strategy or a religious creed, Jesus offers to fix us. To take what is broken and make it whole. To enable rest where none was possible. To do the work we couldn't so we don't have to bear the indomitable weight of life.

Jesus bore our yoke on the cross.

We're invited to take up his yoke in life.

Prayer for today

Jesus, I thank you for your sacrifice. Thank you that it was for me. I trust that when you died on the cross, God was winning my forgiveness, and I accept it today. Thank you for carrying my burdens and offering me rest. Fill me with your rest today.

Amen.

Chapter 5 | The Yoke of the Cross

5.3

It is Finished

When he had received the drink, Jesus said, "It is finished." With that, he bowed his head and gave up his spirit.

John 19:30 NIV

Our whole journey so far finds its climax in these few words and what they say about Jesus' work and his rest.

We understand intuitively that rest comes after work. It's this intuition (mixed with unreasonable stubbornness) which has sometimes led me to renovate our house until the odd hours of the morning. The final coat of paint is rolled on by a half-zombie because a 2am finish is more acceptable than letting a sensible bedtime defer completion. At best, I would find partial rest, disturbed rest—a break until I could attack it again.

But the deep exhale of slumping onto the mattress after a fully accomplished job is a different kind of rest. The latent muscular tension dissolves. The mind is at peace. And then there's the knowledge that there is no more work to do. That's deep rest.

For the Roman soldiers who crucified Jesus, the task would have been unsettling. This man was alleged to be both a king and a criminal. The sign above him reading, 'King of the Jews', seemed violently at odds with the Jewish voices demanding his death. And what would they have made of his ominous last breath?

It is finished.

What exactly, was finished?

The soldiers could not have known that this was the culmination of a divine plan that had been unfolding for thousands of years. Far from a cry of defeat, Jesus was declaring victory.

Far from succumbing to the schemes of evil, Jesus is *entering rest*.

I hear what you're thinking. How can this moment be about rest?

Bear with me—it's glorious.

John's gospel records Jesus saying one Greek word at this moment on the cross: *tetelestai*. This word puts all other words of completion to shame. It was a word of utter finality. The task wasn't just completed—it had been tenaciously pursued to its bitter end, perfected. Nothing could be more accomplished, and nothing more could be accomplished.

Jesus wasn't finished on the cross. *His work was.*

And what was his work? Paying for the sins of the world. Carrying our burdens so we could be given his yoke. He did the work so we could find the rest. In fact, Jesus in this moment is *leading us into rest.*

Jesus alludes to rest at many places during his ministry. But before the cross, rest is not possible. Three chapters before his promise of Soul Rest, Jesus utters the following words:

> *"Foxes have holes, and birds of the air have nests, but the Son of Man has nowhere to lay his head."*
>
> *Matthew 8:20*

His earthly life was one that experienced the same lack of rest we do, only without a burdened soul. There is clearly a future

Chapter 5 | The Yoke of the Cross

point in mind when Jesus promised rest in Matthew 11. But there came a moment where Jesus did feel his soul burdened, and it was necessary for him to both endure and conquer in that moment before he himself could find rest and lead us into it.

Jesus did two things after he said, *tetelestai.*

Firstly, he bowed his head. This may seem a natural physical reflex, but it carries huge symbolic significance. The phrase for 'bowing his head' in the original language occurs in only one other moment in Jesus' life.

Foxes have holes... but the Son of Man has nowhere to *lay his head.*[24]

During his life, Jesus knew that there was no place of true rest for *anyone*, including him, because *his work* was not finished. But on the cross he found a place to lay his head. He could rest because *it was finished.*

Secondly, Jesus gave up his spirit. His spirit was not taken away from him. He did not expire. A more literal translation of the verb *paradidōmi* here is that he 'handed over' his spirit. To whom?

---

[24] Mt 8:20 *tēn kephalēn klinē*

Soul Rest

To God.

Why?

Because that's how we enter rest. We give our spirit, soul, body, our whole selves over to God.

The promise of Soul Rest in Matthew 11 is made possible by the cross. Like the cascading lenses of an optometrist's eye-testing apparatus, the whole picture comes into view at once.

The weight which was upon our souls was our sin. Our life of restlessness and anxiety is our attempt to carry it, to do the work of paying for it. When Jesus promises that he will give us rest, it is by wiping out our burdens. On the cross, he vanquished them with such finality that heaven declared over our burdens: *tetelestai*.

Based on his finished work, Jesus lay down his head and gave over his spirit to God, and he entered rest. And he invites us to do the same. Not because of any accomplishment of our own, but because of Jesus' finished work on our behalf.

For those who accept his offer and take on his yoke, it's that soul-deep feeling of a thud on a soft mattress after a hard day's work. Tension dissolves, peace overwhelms. Our souls are eternally secure. We didn't do it, but he did.

This unburdened life becomes the greatest adventure of discovery. We get to live from rest, not for rest. We were told

Chapter 5 | The Yoke of the Cross

that discovering the world would fulfil us, but oh, how much sweeter it is to discover the one who made it, deeper day by day!

And all we have to do is to accept the trade. Our yoke for his.

So here it is. Soul Rest. Are you in?

Prayer overleaf

Today's prayer is a little different.

If you know for certain that you are a Christian, that your soul is eternally secure in Jesus, skip to the next section. But if you've never been a Christian, or you aren't sure that your soul is totally secure in Jesus, this bit is for you.

The Bible teaches that we can be certain of our salvation in Jesus.

> *Whoever has the Son has life. Whoever does not have the Son of God does not have life.*
>
> *1 John 5:12*

This is the real reason we can exchange the anxiety of a restless soul for one that is full of peace. When we come to Jesus and give our lives to him, our soul is no longer in freefall; it's held eternally secure in Jesus. And that makes all the difference.

> *If you confess with your mouth that Jesus is Lord and believe in your heart that God raised him from the dead, you will be saved. [10] For with the heart one believes and is justified, and with the mouth one confesses and is saved.*
>
> *Romans 10:9-10*

Chapter 5 | The Yoke of the Cross

This is how someone becomes a Christian. Firstly, to confess out loud that Jesus is Lord. Secondly, to believe that God raised him from the dead. That's a choice of faith. And when you believe in the resurrection, you are also believing in everything Jesus did before the resurrection, because if the resurrection is true, all of it is true.

So, here it is. Soul Rest is on the table. It's yours to receive. Pray:

> God, thank you for sending Jesus to die for me. Thank you that on the cross, he paid for my sin and took upon himself the burden of my hurts, pain, sickness, disappointments, and failures.
>
> I'm sorry that I have lived a life that has at times rejected you. I'm sorry that I've attempted to run my own life, and I acknowledge that you are Lord.
>
> Please take my heart. I entrust my whole self to you and accept you as my Lord. Please enter into my heart and bring rest for my soul. I accept your yoke today. I confess you as my Lord.
>
> Amen.

One last thing: find yourself in church this Sunday. God will meet you there and so will his people. This is not a step you were meant to take alone, and much of the beauty of knowing Jesus is found in being with his people.

If you know Jesus

Knowing Jesus is a now-and-not-yet experience. There is a moment where your sins are forgiven eternally, your life secured and all the promises of Scripture are written beside your name in heaven. But in this life, they can only feel partial.

Without becoming a Christian, no-one can find Soul Rest. But that first and important experience is only the starting point for pursuing Jesus in this life. We need to be continually brought back to the beauty of the gospel, seeing it in new light and letting it inform our life, not just our beliefs.

The inescapable reality of following Jesus is that the degree to which all his promises find themselves fulfilled in our experience corresponds with how seriously we take his commands. So, do you take him seriously? If it meant a greater sense of peace and rest in your life, would you make the changes he asks you to? Will the years to come in your life be better than the years before?

The concept of a 'recommitment' is a powerful step in the Christian journey. It is akin to a 'renewal of vows' in a marriage. It doesn't undermine what has come before but declares that your commitment to God is renewed. Why not recommit your life to him today?

Chapter 5 | The Yoke of the Cross

5.4
Weekly Reflection

Is there anything in my life, beliefs, or experience of rest which has changed in the last 5 weeks?

_____

_____

_____

_____

_____

_____

_____

_____

_____

Chapter 5 | The Yoke of the Cross

On a scale of 1 to 10, with 1 being the furthest away and 10 being the closest, how close do you/did you feel to God at these points:

Before this course began: _____

Now: _____

What are the specific burdens in my life I would like to hand over to Jesus?

_____

_____

_____

_____

_____

_____

_____

_____

_____

_____

Pray and listen for God to speak to you about these burdens. What does he say? How is he asking you to view these burdens in light of the finished work of the cross?

_____

_____

_____

_____

_____

_____

_____

_____

_____

Is he encouraging you to adopt a different perspective?

Is he asking you to do something differently, or initiate a conversation with someone?

Chapter 5 | The Yoke of the Cross

Write down anything you sense God might be saying to you:

_____

_____

_____

_____

_____

_____

_____

_____

_____

_____

_____

_____

_____

_____

_____

5.5

Group Session

This week we have examined the yoke which Jesus bore on our behalf. In carrying the cross, Jesus carried the burden which was always meant to be ours. Every pain, weight, anxiety, and fear we feel in this life was placed upon Jesus on the cross, and in his death, the burden was fully consumed.

It is exactly because Jesus took our burden that we are invited to take his. And the difference is night and day. Our burden of sin exists to take us all the way to the grave, but his yoke is easy, and his burden is light. It's only once we see our burdens laid upon him and taken to the grave that we can feel them shed permanently from our shoulders.

The even better news is that Jesus didn't stay dead. He was buried on Good Friday but rose on Easter Sunday. His resurrected life is the very same life we are invited to, and now that his work is finished, the gates are open.

Chapter 5 | The Yoke of the Cross

DISCUSSION QUESTIONS

1. What did you think of the readings this week?

2. What stood out to you the most?

3. Reflect with each other on your Soul Rest journey so far.

4. What has changed in your life?

5. What has not changed, but you would like it to?

This is a special week. The key to Soul Rest is found in placing our faith in Jesus and his finished work on the cross. For the person who makes this decision with their life, there could be no greater shift in the health of their soul. The difference is not so much from sick to healthy as it is from dead to alive—and being made alive is worth celebrating!

Plan as a group to be at your local church this Sunday. There you will be able to celebrate with the local gathering of God's people what God has been doing in your lives and others.

Pray for one another:

- To see and feel burdens relieved at the cross
- That God would continue the good work begun this week

A BRIEF NOTE ABOUT BAPTISM

In the New Testament, Baptism always accompanies faith. The first thing that the new Christians on the day of Pentecost are told is to:

> *"Repent and **be baptized** every one of you in the name of Jesus Christ for the forgiveness of your sins, and you will receive the gift of the Holy Spirit."*
>
> Acts 2:38

Baptism is a public declaration of faith and the ceremony (or rite) of initiation in the Church. It has great symbolic significance, with the waters indicating a spiritual washing and purifying, and the immersion in water indicating our old self dying with Jesus and being raised out of the grave with him.

If you have decided to trust Jesus with your life, accept his yoke and receive his Soul Rest, baptism is for you. This weekend is the perfect time to do it. Let your group leader know if you would like to be baptised this weekend, and they can explain the process to you. The local church will be ready and delighted to baptise you.

If you have further questions about baptism or you're not yet ready, arrange to catch up with your group leader to discuss what it means.

Chapter 5 | The Yoke of the Cross

Soul Rest

Chapter 6
Soul Rest

6.1

A New Master

No one can serve two masters. Either you will hate the one and love the other, or you will be devoted to the one and despise the other. You cannot serve both God and money.

Matthew 6:24 NIV

Demons come back.

Jesus had a lot to do with demons. If you read through Mark's gospel, you would be convinced that he was writing a blockbuster script, *Jesus: Demon Slayer*. Wherever he goes, the unclean spirits shudder and flee, bowing to his personal authority like a lead weight obeys the law of gravity.

Jesus explains that when a demon is cast out, it wanders, homeless, before returning to its old 'haunt'. There it finds the place "empty, swept, and put in order."[25] Then, like the cobbler's pegs you thought you removed from your garden, it grabs seven of its buddies and invades the space once more, until "the last state of that person is worse than the first."[26]

Even if you don't believe in demonic spirits, people often speak figuratively of their own demons—the subversive and intangible powers that negatively affect their life. They may be old family secrets, regrets of an earlier life, or the demons of addiction. Everybody is *battling their own demons.*

Most of us are acutely aware that these demons can rear their head at awkward and unwanted moments. Even from a place of consistent victory, we fear that if they return, our resolve would be no match. One sip of the drink, one accidental click, and we're losing the war again.

When Jesus says it's impossible to serve two masters, he's referring to the same dynamic. Only one master can be present in the house at a time. It's one thing to kick out the old master, and it's another to install the new. If we fail to

---

[25] Matthew 12:44
[26] Matthew 12:45

welcome the new master, the old comes back with a vengeance.

How is your detox going, by the way?

The spiritual detox is essentially an exercise in kicking out the old master, 'exorcising the demons.' I hope you have started to notice some differences in your life for the better. But removing the problem is only half the solution. Whatever you have detoxed from in your life needs to be replaced with something fruitful and life-giving.

You need to welcome the new master into that space.

There are two facets to this. The first is spiritual, and the second is practical. Firstly, whatever you have gained through your detox needs to be given to God in your heart. If you've gained more time (which I hope you have), then that time needs to be offered to God. Acknowledge in your heart that he is the master of that time, and he can direct how you should spend it.

If you think that kicking out the old master has given you more life to spend how you want, then it's only a matter of time before the demons come back.

If you've gained emotional resilience, greater mental health, a sense of freedom, or better physical health, then it needs to be offered to God. He's the one who won it for you, and it should be offered back to him.

Take a moment to think what it is that you have gained. Now consider if you're willing to offer it back to him.

Pray now simply to do so.

Secondly, you need to implement a practical placeholder for the lordship of Jesus into that space. It won't be enough to simply say, 'it's yours', for the same reason that offering my wife a coffee means nothing until she's sipping sweet caffeine from my Italian-made machine.

We're talking about spiritual disciplines again. But at this point, we have the context to understand why they are so vitally important.

Jesus is asking for your time. I could guarantee an accurate measure of your sense of intimacy with God through just one question:

How much of your time is spent with God?

Giving God your time by practicing spiritual disciplines is how we stamp his lordship on our lives. It's how we establish him as the new master of the house once the old is gone. It's how we ensure the demons don't come back.

Everyone faces their own struggles in making this work. Your life will look different to mine, and to the others in your group, both in the behaviours that compete for your time, and the disciplines which feed your soul.

In my life, this works out to a very simple equation. The daily competition is between prayer and my phone:

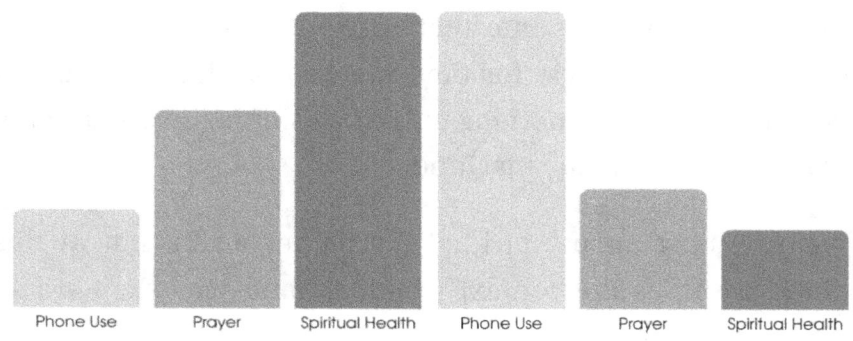

My phone isn't evil. But the equation is so clear that it may as well be.

The trick to getting this equation to work is that your spiritual disciplines must fill your soul. Empty Bible reading is like eating bubbles. You're not sure why you're doing it, and it doesn't fill you up. Prayer without connection to God is like rolling a lawn mower over your grass without starting it. It achieves nothing but sweat and frustration.

This equation only worked for me once I learned to love prayer. Ten years ago, the spiritual discipline that most filled my soul was reading my Bible, because I loved doing it (and still do). The reason I love both these things is because I have discovered how to know, listen to and connect with God through them.

It's natural for these disciplines to change through seasons of our life. Don't assume that what filled you when you were young will do the job as seasons, pressures and circumstances change. These disciplines are only a vessel for connection with God.

Your top priority now is to discover and implement at least one spiritual discipline which genuinely connects you to God and fills your soul. It will require some reflecting on your personality, understanding your time and opportunities, and looking to the lives of others for inspiration.

Prayer for today

God, I thank you for the ground I have gained back in my life. I understand that I need you and that means I need to be with you. I know that you have made my soul and understand it intimately. Show me what spiritual disciplines will best feed my soul and help me to fill my life with them for your sake.

Amen.

6.2

When You Pray

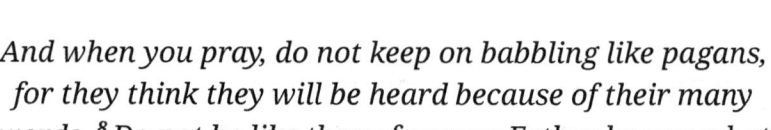

And when you pray, do not keep on babbling like pagans, for they think they will be heard because of their many words. ⁸ Do not be like them, for your Father knows what you need before you ask him.

Matthew 6:7-8 NIV

There are two types of Christians. Those who love prayer and those who find their faith characterized by frequent and painful struggles.

Prayers and strugglers.

(I know you had to read that twice)

Which kind are you?

No-one has ever truly discovered the easy yoke of Jesus without also discovering the life-giving beauty and mystery of prayer. Believe me, it is both of those things. Anyone who has prayed has had to wrestle with the notion that a God who claims to hear our prayers seems to leave many unanswered.

Those who love prayer do not find themselves immune from struggle but equipped for it. The struggle does not characterize their faith; the provision of God does.

I enjoy finding Christian writers, speakers and thinkers, both modern and ancient. Every so often, I stumble upon someone whose works are so captivating that they seem to drip with the sweet grace of Jesus himself. I binge their content on YouTube, devour their biographies or books, and spend a season admiring their faith. Inevitably, one consistent element of their personal lives sticks out.

Prayer.

Every single one will talk about prayer like a precious jewel, a thirst-quenching well, a soothing balm, or the most intimate friend. They don't just find prayer important; they love it.

That was not my experience growing up. Prayer was an unwanted duty which I was told would make me healthy, like the rejected vegetables on my plate. The concept of actually enjoying prayer never crossed my mind.

Slowly, the truth became undeniable. Prayer is the secret ingredient to intimacy with God. And intimacy with God through prayer inevitably results in an influential life. Prayer isn't the bitter medicine of the spiritual diet most of us believe it to be; it is the sweetest of invitations of Jesus.

Then it clicked.

Without a love for prayer, my Christian life was being wasted.

Too many jaded Christians live an unsatisfied life. Decades of hard experiences cause them to shake their fists at God in confusion as peace, joy and love remain like a carrot dangled on a stick, deceptive eternal promises, a marketing ploy for their obedience in this life. Yet the key to experiencing abundant life lies for most of us unopened on our doorstep.

A life of vibrant, relational, intimate prayer.

Prayer is the Prince of spiritual disciplines.

It transcends personality type, age, circumstance, access to resources, and fuels every other marker of spiritual health. You don't need anything to pray. It is simply a hotline from your heart to God's ear.

Even those who don't have a faith are moved to the simple and natural reflex of crying out to our Maker. Research shows that while only 53% of Australians consider themselves Christian,

60% of the population admits to praying.[27] Prayer isn't fundamentally a religious activity—it's a human one.

No wonder so many of history's most potent Christians came out of the monastic movement, a life built around prayer. But if there is any wisdom from the monks concerning how to pray or what it should look like, it's only because they learned it from Jesus.

Jesus' life of perfect connection with God was saturated with prayer. We know that his habit was to withdraw to desolate places to pray, because it was there that he could shut out the noise of the world and find himself in the presence of God.

Jesus' teaching on prayer didn't start with, 'If you pray…' He said, "When you pray…" He assumes you are praying. There is no greater oxymoron than a Christian who doesn't pray. If it so important to the practice of faith, why shouldn't we love it? A sailor loves to sail. A runner loves to run. A Christian loves to pray.

Why?

Learning to love prayer is learning to love God.

This world does not want you to love God. It will fill your time and your head with busyness and noise which make prayer

---

[27] https://www.ncls.org.au/articles/how-religious-are-australians/

impossible. Every one of us has a fight on our hands to sanctify our time and give it to God, to be continually in relationship with him through prayer.

There is plenty of content out there which can give far more detail and justification than I could attempt in this one reading. I will suggest some and recommend you go looking for prayer resources. But here are the perspective-shifting truths which I found critical to developing a love for prayer:

1. **Prayer is not duty but relationship.** Jesus taught us to pray to 'Our Father', implying a sense of the closest possible relationship. No relationship was ever sustained by silence. If you haven't found your prayer life to be relational, you haven't yet discovered prayer.
2. **Prayer is not only about speaking to God but listening to him.** God speaks. Ask him a question and then wait. See if he prompts a thought or leads your heart or directs you to a verse of Scripture. Discovering a lively conversation with God is crucial to learning to love prayer.
3. **Prayer requires time and silence.** God speaks in a whisper. You won't hear him if your environment or your own brain is full of noise. Mums of young kids—I see you. Those seem like the only things your life cannot accommodate. Hang in there. Do whatever it takes to find time and silence and don't fill all of it

with chores or scrolling or other duties. It's possibly the hardest season in this respect, but it is worth it if you can make it work.
4. **You don't have to be 'good at prayer'.** Jesus spoke directly against those who thought that God might hear them more because of their lengthy, ornate or powerfully worded prayers. Like a father lying next to his child at bedtime, God just wants to hear your voice.

Lastly, there is only one way to learn how to pray: by praying. Do it messily. Do it with all your awkwardness and apprehension. Be vulnerable with God. Ask him to teach you how to pray. If you do, I promise that you will be taking him up on one of the most life-giving offers this side of eternity.

If you find a love for prayer, you will find a love for God.

Prayer for today

Dear God, I thank you that you have given us a way to talk to you and experience your presence. I recognize that the pressures of this life are working against me having an intimate relationship with you. Help me to find a love for prayer. Show me one small step I can make to find you in prayer. Teach me to hear your voice.

Amen.

Soul Rest

If you would like to read more on prayer, here are some excellent modern books:

How to Pray: a simple guide for normal people, by Pete Greig

Praying Like Monks, Living Like Fools, by Tyler Staton

Red Moon Rising, by Pete Greig and Dave Roberts

You could also try Pete Grieg's *Prayer Course:*

prayercourse.org

Chapter 6 | Soul Rest

6.3

Soul Rest

"Teacher, which is the greatest commandment in the Law?"
³⁷ Jesus replied: "'Love the Lord your God with all your heart and with all your soul and with all your mind.' ³⁸ This is the first and greatest commandment."

Matthew 22:36-38 NIV

A soul at rest loves God.

When Jesus promised that those who took his yoke upon them would find rest for their souls, he had this commandment in mind. This isn't one of the Ten Commandments given to Moses, but neither did Jesus make it up. In fact, this commandment is given as a *prerequisite* to Israel's keeping of the Ten:

Chapter 6 | Soul Rest

> *Hear, O Israel: The Lord our God, the Lord is one. ⁵ Love the Lord your God with all your heart and with all your soul and with all your strength. ⁶ These commandments [the Ten] that I give you today are to be on your hearts.*
>
> *Deuteronomy 6:4-6 NIV*

The rest of God's law cannot be kept without the starting point: love God.

So, do you love God?

How do you view him? Is he a distant, omnipotent being behind a set of ornate silver gates? Is he a wrathful, judgmental deity with a lightning bolt poised in one hand? Is he a wrinkly old man with a look of disapproval hiding behind an ancient beard?

Could anyone love such a God?

Or is he like Jesus reveals himself to be—gentle and lowly, a friend to sinners, full of compassion and mercy wrapped in divine strength and power?

Jesus had a constant feud with the religious leaders of his day. The reason was they got God all wrong—and surprisingly (or maybe not), most of our modern world perpetuates their exact misunderstanding. Shortly after this encounter in Matthew

22, Jesus says that these religious teachers "tie up heavy burdens" and "lay them upon people's shoulders".[28]

He's using the yoke imagery again.

The heavy burden of the religious teachers was a list of dos and don'ts, additions to the law which said, 'you can only find favour with God if you earn it.' Our world is still confused in the same way. Religion is about what you can and can't do. Everyone is trying to earn their way to heaven through doing right and being good.

But the yoke of Jesus is expressed in this one magisterial commandment: love God.

I've been through various seasons of church attendance in my life. At times, my obsession with going to church might be seen as fanaticism—twice on Sunday, a midweek Bible study, a morning prayer meeting, a Friday night youth group. But at other times, attendance has been hard.

Like many people, I've left churches because of broken relationships. I've fought with my spouse while getting kids ready early on a Sunday to feel like the effort wasn't worth it.

---

[28] Matthew 23:4

I've experienced church services which filled me, and some that left me confused and lonely.

One thing keeps me coming back. It's not the friends I attend with, how much I like the service, or how convenient the overall experience is. It's not the fact that I couldn't find other important and satisfying things to do on a Sunday, like head to the beach, get involved in sports, or enjoy local markets and cafes. It's not because some deep cultural tie compels me to do it for nostalgia or in memory of my grandma.

It's God. I love him.

It's the same reason I've learned to love prayer. I've discovered how prayer connects me to the one in whom my soul delights.

It's the same reason I spent six months in my twenties devouring the Scriptures for hours daily. I heard the voice of the one who made my soul and calls me to himself.

It's the same reason the boy Jesus, after being missing for three days, was found in the temple and declared to his bewildered parents, "Wouldn't you know I *had to be in my Father's house?*"[29]

---

[29] Luke 2:49

Soul Rest

The reason Jesus lived a life of constant Soul Rest was because he was the only one who ever managed to love God with his whole soul, his whole mind, and all of his strength. And if you're going to truly find Soul Rest, you need to learn to love God.

For those who've grown up with a skeptical view of religion or a negative view of the church, this seems foreign and maybe even bizarre. Or maybe it's the one thing that finally makes sense. Here is the secret to faith: Christianity is more than just doing stuff and believing stuff. It is a personal relationship with the God who knows you better than yourself and is filled with love for you.

This final week is about finding spiritual disciplines which fill your soul and using them as a placeholder to mark the lordship of Jesus over your time. But deeper than that, it's about loving God. When these activities breathe divine life into you, they are no chore.

So, now it's up to you. Make it your mission to find God through meaningful and regular disciplines. Cast aside as many pieces of your complex life as necessary to make a path for God to get to your soul. Make prayer, church, and reading your Bible a priority.

Love God. Do it properly. Do it with your whole soul. Put all your strength and your mind into loving him.

Make every opportunity to know and connect with him count. Pursue them like your eternity depends on it. Give him more of your time than you ever thought you would and see how he repays you in love.

Find Soul Rest.

6.4

Weekly Reflection

Here is a list of spiritual disciplines, or ways of connecting with God. There are lots of ways to categorise spiritual disciplines, or even to decide what makes it on the list. The New Testament teaches a host of practices that are critical to the Christian life. This list will not exhaust them. I have placed the ones which, in my opinion and experience, most tangibly connect us to the presence of God.

'The Big 5' are what I would class as essential Christian practices and have a Scriptural mandate attached to them. Many of the others are also commanded by Scripture, and some are implied or observed.

Many of them are deep concepts of their own and will require further research to understand them. Perhaps a good starting point would be to ask your group about their experience with the ones that interest you.

THE BIG 5:

- Prayer (1 Thessalonians 5:17)
- Bible reading (Colossians 3:16)
- Gathering in Christian community: Church (Hebrews 10:25)
- Worship (Colossians 3:16)
- Sabbath (Mark 2:27)

MORE BROADLY:

- Solitude
- Fasting
- Journalling
- Appreciating God in nature
- Study
- Contemplation
- Simplicity
- Art and creativity
- Witness (Matthew 28:19)
- Generosity (1 Timothy 6:18)
- Service (Galatians 5:13)
- Confession (James 5:16)

It may take some serious thought and perseverance to get it to work. Plan to give it a red-hot go, and if one of them doesn't hit the mark for you, try another one. Connecting with God is worth the effort.

Soul Rest

What has worked for me previously and is it still working?

_____

_____

_____

_____

_____

Which other practices am I drawn to?

_____

_____

_____

_____

_____

_____

How does the idea of 'loving God' make me feel?

6.5

Group Session

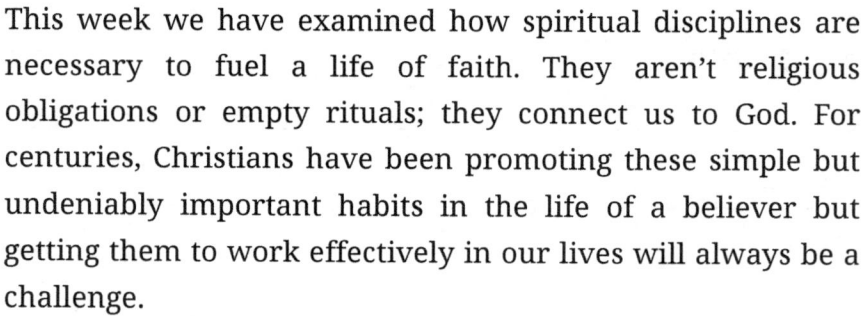

This week we have examined how spiritual disciplines are necessary to fuel a life of faith. They aren't religious obligations or empty rituals; they connect us to God. For centuries, Christians have been promoting these simple but undeniably important habits in the life of a believer but getting them to work effectively in our lives will always be a challenge.

To have any success in implementing spiritual disciplines, we must have a grasp on how important they are. We must also understand that there are forces at work in the world around us which actively seek to pull us away from these life-giving practices. Every one of us has a fight on our hands for our own soul health.

Chapter 6 | Soul Rest

DISCUSSION QUESTIONS

1. How did you find the week's readings?

2. What stood out to you?

3. How would you describe your love for God?

4. How would you describe your prayer life?

5. What has been your experience of spiritual disciplines?

6. Which of the spiritual disciplines attracts you the most?

7. What would you say has changed most for you over the course?

8. What would you like your spiritual life to look like moving forward?

Maintaining Momentum

If you came as an existing group, continue supporting each other in implementing healthy practices in your life.

If your group has formed for the purpose of this course, you may like to consider continuing to meet. If you need any help or guidance, please get in touch with your local ministry team who will be happy to provide you with resources.

Pray for each other:

- To celebrate the fruit over the course
- To discover an intimate, personal connection with God
- To grow in a life-long journey of faith

Chapter 6 | Soul Rest

6.6
Where to from here?

It's human nature to search for a quick fix. From instant creams to pyramid schemes, our attempts to better our lives continually prove there is no shortcut to health and success.

This journey is not a shortcut. No quick fix exists to living a life of spiritual meaning and significance. This is why Jesus frames his offer of rest with the language of pursuit, "come to me..." (Matthew 11:28). These six weeks are designed to be a starter motor for your life of faith, a high-voltage injection to keep the powerful regular motor running.

We have landed in essentially a simple, historically proven place when it comes to following Jesus. God is not interested in a new gospel or a savvy perspective to draw us to follow him. It is simply about contextualising the once-received faith of the saints to the complex modern lives we live. This faith unavoidably includes three behaviours that our society and our flesh are desperate to erode: prayer, reading the Bible and attending church.

Many of us have never trusted that these fuel our soul. Either we have come from a place of scepticism, no faith, or a different faith and these appear as religious agenda, or we have done our best to make them work but still feel unsatisfied and potentially distant from God.

You may even still be sceptical that this is all a ploy to get you to church regularly. I accept that there's no way around that perception. I only wish people would understand how regular, weekly (not monthly) church attendance is good for your soul.

In my experience, there are two ways to discover these practices, or find our way back to them meaningfully. The first is some kind of spiritual circuit-breaker. Something dramatic flips a switch in our hearts and we suddenly take these matters seriously. God often builds uncomfortable circuit-breakers into our lives to gain our attention through health episodes or other difficult circumstances. He's not being malignant. Our choices are often incompatible with reality and God temporarily allows them to break for our benefit.

The second pathway is through a compelling presentation of the 'why' behind good spiritual habits. I hope this journey is both. The end point, then, of this journey should be considered like a highway on-ramp. If you have brought your spiritual life up to speed, it's now about merging onto the road of life-long spiritual growth.

The journey to effective spiritual disciplines has often been called a 'rule of life.' There are many great resources out there on this concept. To express my understanding simply and practically, it is the choice to build your life around a commitment to spiritual disciplines that work for your faith. Monasteries articulated 'a rule' which is essentially their daily routine and way of life. These communities were born when an individual's Christian Walk became so compelling that others chose to mimic them. Although we don't tend to create formal communities of spirituality this way anymore, our interconnected world presents us with a great opportunity. We have the flexibility to form our own 'rule', borrowing as much or as little from others as fits into our lives.

Here are some pieces of my 'rule':

I set an alarm for the same time every day, and no matter where I am or what I am doing, I stop and pray. It usually lasts about five minutes and consists of simple prayers of relationship, offering myself to God and inviting him to interrupt my life. This has been transformative in my love for prayer and experience of God daily.

I choose to be busy but not feel busy. Like you, I'm not wired for constant meditation and relaxation. Working fills my soul. But I choose not to *feel* busy. When people ask me how my week has been, I never respond with 'busy'. Objectively, I probably am, but I don't want busyness to be my schedule's defining feature. I have found that describing my day-to-day in other ways makes me feel less frantic and better able to cope with high demands. Of course, this doesn't replace an active and diligent management of my overall load.

I have deliberate boundaries on my phone use. It's never the first thing I use in the morning or the last at night, and use app restriction tools. Often, I use a grey-scale filter which limits the addictive responses of my brain when using it.

Finding a 'rule' which works for you is one of the joys of having a unique and individual relationship with God. Don't try and do something too big too quickly. Choose something simple and achievable and ask God for help. He will grow it to what he wants. I look forward to my practices growing with my faith and adapting to match different seasons of life.

My prayer for you through this imperfect and limited offering to God is that you would find renewed motivation and power in your pursuit of him, that you would hear his call to give him more of your time and devotion, and that you would experience the flow of abundant life Jesus has promised.

"I came that they may have life, and have it abundantly"

John 10:10

Acknowledgements

The Kingdom of God is a wonderful place, and very few things of value are done without the combined effort of God's people. First thanks for this material goes to Pat Hegarty, whose collection of six-week courses provided the template for this one. Additionally, his leadership is what saw the need for a course like this and gave me the guidance, encouragement and confidence to meet the need.

I have the unique privilege of being married to a copy editor, so immense gratitude belongs to my wife, Bek, who not only extended patience during this project, but edited every word. She is ultimately responsible for anything of quality that is found on these pages.

A heartfelt nod goes to my colleague and friend, Liam Berry. In addition to the cover design, he has graciously let me interrupt his own significant load constantly to read a chapter, solve an IT issue, and provide helpful feedback.

Three other influences should be mentioned. The late Tim Keller told of how when he moved to New York, he needed to re-envision the gospel for his city. How did the timeless message of Jesus Christ meet the pain that he saw around him? It was this question which inspired me to grow a heart for the city of Brisbane and drove me to the heart of Matthew 11, where Jesus promises us Soul Rest.

John Mark Comer's book, *The Ruthless Elimination of Hurry*, has had a significant impact on my personal faith, and many of the concepts in this material were first made clear to me through his book. Those who have read his work will find a similar flavour here, applied to the Australian context, because I believe that Australians deserve ministry that speaks directly to their hearts.

I could not have attempted to write anything of value in this space without developing a personal love for prayer, and in that regard, the testimony and works of Tyler Staton have been influential for me. In particular, no book has described the beauty of prayer with such allure as his, *Praying Like Monks, Living Like Fools*.

Finally, God is worthy of far more than this work of devotion could achieve. May He use it for his glory.

Soul Rest

www.ingramcontent.com/pod-product-compliance
Lightning Source LLC
Chambersburg PA
CBHW072001290426
44109CB00018B/2088